S. Hrg. 113–628

#BringBackOurGirls: ADDRESSING THE THREAT OF BOKO HARAM

HEARING

BEFORE THE

SUBCOMMITTEE ON AFRICAN AFFAIRS

OF THE

COMMITTEE ON FOREIGN RELATIONS
UNITED STATES SENATE

ONE HUNDRED THIRTEENTH CONGRESS

SECOND SESSION

MAY 15, 2014

Printed for the use of the Committee on Foreign Relations

Available via the World Wide Web: http://www.gpo.gov/fdsys/

U.S. GOVERNMENT PUBLISHING OFFICE

94–293 PDF   WASHINGTON : 2015

For sale by the Superintendent of Documents, U.S. Government Publishing Office
Internet: bookstore.gpo.gov   Phone: toll free (866) 512–1800; DC area (202) 512–1800
Fax: (202) 512–2104   Mail: Stop IDCC, Washington, DC 20402–0001

COMMITTEE ON FOREIGN RELATIONS

ROBERT MENENDEZ, New Jersey, *Chairman*

BARBARA BOXER, California
BENJAMIN L. CARDIN, Maryland
JEANNE SHAHEEN, New Hampshire
CHRISTOPHER A. COONS, Delaware
RICHARD J. DURBIN, Illinois
TOM UDALL, New Mexico
CHRISTOPHER MURPHY, Connecticut
TIM KAINE, Virginia
EDWARD J. MARKEY, Massachusetts

BOB CORKER, Tennessee
JAMES E. RISCH, Idaho
MARCO RUBIO, Florida
RON JOHNSON, Wisconsin
JEFF FLAKE, Arizona
JOHN McCAIN, Arizona
JOHN BARRASSO, Wyoming
RAND PAUL, Kentucky

DANIEL E. O'BRIEN, *Staff Director*
LESTER E. MUNSON III, *Republican Staff Director*

———————

SUBCOMMITTEE ON AFRICAN AFFAIRS

CHRISTOPHER A. COONS, Delaware, *Chairman*

RICHARD J. DURBIN, Illinois
BENJAMIN L. CARDIN, Maryland
JEANNE SHAHEEN, New Hampshire
TOM UDALL, New Mexico

JEFF FLAKE, Arizona
JOHN McCAIN, Arizona
JOHN BARRASSO, Wyoming
RAND PAUL, Kentucky

(II)

CONTENTS

#BringBackOurGirls: ADDRESSING THE THREAT OF BOKO HARAM

U.S. SENATE,
SUBCOMMITTEE ON AFRICAN AFFAIRS,
COMMITTEE ON FOREIGN RELATIONS,
Washington, DC.

The subcommittee met, pursuant to notice, at 10:04 a.m., in room SD–419, Dirksen Senate Office Building, Hon. Christopher A. Coons (chairman of the subcommittee) presiding.

Present: Senators Coons, Menendez, Cardin, Shaheen, Flake, Rubio, and Barrasso.

OPENING STATEMENT OF HON. CHRISTOPHER A. COONS, U.S. SENATOR FROM DELAWARE

Senator COONS. Good morning. I would like to call to order this hearing of the African Affairs Subcommittee of the Senate Foreign Relations Committee.

Good morning. Exactly 1 month ago today, extremists in northern Nigeria abducted nearly 300 schoolgirls in an unconscionable act of terror. The leaders of the group responsible, Boko Haram, are selling the girls into marriages, forcibly converting them to Islam, and using them as a bargaining chip in negotiations with the Nigerian Government. It is believed the girls are today being held in a dense tropical forest area roughly the size of West Virginia that straddles a porous and ungoverned border with three countries.

Despite being forewarned of a possible attack, reports indicate the local and central government did nothing to protect them when told an attack was imminent. Parents should not have to be afraid to send their children to school, no child should live through the horror these girls have experienced, and no family should have to confront these threats alone.

Unfortunately, these are not the only families who have suffered at the hands of Boko Haram. The same day as these abductions, 75 more people were killed and 100 wounded in a bombing at a bus station in the Nigerian capital city of Abuja. More than 300 people were murdered during a Boko Haram attack in Gamboru just last week. According to Amnesty International, Boko Haram has killed more than 4,000 over the last 3 years, including 1,500 people in the last year alone.

I want to welcome my partner in the Africa Subcommittee, Senator Flake, as well as Chairman Menendez, Ranking Member Corker, and other members, as we look at the response to these kidnappings and consider the grave and growing threat presented by Boko Haram.

This subcommittee last met to consider conditions in Nigeria in 2012, when we looked at the persistent divides between the north and south in economic potential, governance, education, and social services, and the very real security challenges created by these differences. Nigeria is an important partner in the region, but Boko Haram has capitalized on pervasive corruption, poor governance, and growing poverty in the north to undermine domestic and regional stability.

Boko Haram, whose name means ''Western Education is Sinful,'' targets public institutions, churches, and schools, and children are the frequent victims of its vicious attacks. As New York Times columnist Kristof wrote, just last weekend, ''The greatest threat to extremism is not drones firing missiles, but girls reading books.'' The schoolgirls from Chibok in Nigeria demonstrated great courage, returning to their school to take their final exams in the face of an explicit terrorist threat, a group that targeted them simply because they sought an education.

Boko Haram is trying to send a message, and the world, starting with the Nigerian Government, must respond by saying their crimes will not be tolerated and perpetrators held accountable.

We are holding this hearing, in part, because of the outpouring of concern from many of my constituents and millions of Americans. The #BringBackOurGirls hash tag, which some pundits have mocked, has been mentioned more than 3 million times on Twitter, and those Tweets, posts on Facebook, Instagram, and others, were from people trying to get our attention and trying to make sure the United States is doing everything it reasonably can to help the Nigerians bring these abducted girls home. Those people deserve to know that we hear you and share your goals.

Every day these girls are missing, it becomes less likely they will be returned home safely. It took too long for the Nigerian government to respond to these girls' abduction. It took too long for the Nigerian Government to accept offers of assistance from the United States, the United Kingdom, France, and China. And, once accepted, it took too long for that assistance to be implemented. I am glad a U.S. team is on the ground now, and we need to make sure not another day is wasted. We cannot stand by while Boko Haram viciously attacks Nigerian citizens, their freedom, their security, and their right to an education.

So, in this hearing, we will discuss the response of the Nigerian Government to Boko Haram both before and after the abduction; we will consider what the United States is doing, and can do, to help in response to the abductions and in confronting Boko Haram; finally, we will consider the regional implications of this growing threat and what action can and should be taken by Cameroon, Chad, and Niger to ensure the schoolgirls are not taken across borders and to minimize the growing regional threat.

With that, I would like to invite an opening statement by my ranking Senator Flake and then a statement by the full-committee chairman, Senator Menendez.

Senator Flake.

3

OPENING STATEMENT OF HON. JEFF FLAKE, U.S. SENATOR FROM ARIZONA

Senator FLAKE. Thank you, Mr. Chairman. Thanks for calling this hearing.

Appreciate the witnesses coming forward. I look forward to their testimony. I will not take any time here, just to say that I agree with the chairman's comments. We want to know what the U.S. Government is doing, what the Nigerians have asked for, whether we can help them, or not, in this regard.

So, I look forward to the testimony, and thank you for calling the hearing.

Senator COONS. Thank you, Senator. And I greatly appreciate your cooperation and real partnership in working on this subcommittee.

To the full-committee chairman, Senator Menendez.

Senator.

STATEMENT OF HON. ROBERT MENENDEZ, U.S. SENATOR FROM NEW JERSEY

The CHAIRMAN. Well, thank you, Mr. Chairman.

As I sit here in your chair, I get the Blue Hen vibrations coming from Delaware.

So, I appreciate your and Senator Flake's leadership on the Africa Subcommittee on a wide range of topics. And today is a continuation of that leadership. And we are all thankful for the work that you do on behalf of all of us who serve on the committee. So, thank you for your work and your leadership.

It is very rare, I should say, that I come to a subcommittee hearing. As a matter of fact, I have not done it in the 17 months that I have been the chairman. I remember Senator Lugar used to do it quite often. But, this is one that I clearly feel compelled to be a part of.

We are all appalled at the plight of nearly 300 young women abducted in Nigeria by Boko Haram, which has been said many times. To me, it is amazing that the phrase "education is forbidden," in the 21st century, is still a reality. Of course, it is a phrase that is counterintuitive to those of us who care about the future of the next generation.

Right now, these girls are separated from their families and no doubt are terrified. I have seen the video released by Boko Haram this week, and my thoughts, as a father, are with the missing girls and their parents.

Frankly, in my view, the fact that incidents like this are happening at all in the 21st century should be deeply troubling to every human being. We must reaffirm and recommit ourselves to the fundamental rule of law everywhere. As parents, as human beings, we must insist that women and girls be treated with dignity and allowed to live and learn in safety from extremists everywhere.

Sadly, while the scale of this incident is staggering, the Boko Haram threat is not a new one. They have led an escalating campaign of atrocities against their own people for 5 years. They are extremists with a gangster mentality who represent no interest but their own, targeting young women, also young men, churches, and schools. I believe they do not represent Islam, and, in my view, their actions cannot go unanswered.

The mothers, activists, and concerned citizens who have taken their outrage and grief to the streets of Abuja, London, and Washington, and the electronic highways of Twitter and Facebook, deserve credit for focusing the world's attention on this crisis and insisting to the Nigerian Government, ''Bring them home.'' Just this past Friday, I joined outraged citizens in my own State of New Jersey, who added their voices to the chorus and took up the cause on social media.

That said, despite offers of assistance from the United States and other international partners, the Nigerian Government's response to this crisis has been tragically and unacceptably slow. I have called on President Jonathan to demonstrate the leadership his nation is demanding. My understanding is that our team of U.S. technical advisors is now on the ground, supporting existing teams, conducting aerial surveillance, and sharing commercial satellite imagery with Nigerian authorities. Beyond what is happening on the ground as we speak, I look forward to hearing our witnesses discuss a plan of action for coordinating with Nigeria over the coming days and weeks.

Finally, from a 30,000-foot view, the rise of groups like Boko Haram do not occur in a vacuum. Nigeria has a long history of division along ethnic and religious lines, tensions that terrorists capitalize on by creating more distrust and more tension. But, as much as we are appalled by the actions of Boko Haram and their tactical effort to use societal fissures to create chaos and distrust, we should also be troubled by a record of excessive force and human rights abuses by Nigeria's military.

I am pleased to see, Mr. Chairman, that you have added an additional witness, Miss Lantana Abdullahi, who has worked in Nigeria on interfaith violence prevention and community reconciliation issues, and has brought together civil society groups, government leaders, and security forces to prevent human rights abuses in Nigeria. And we look forward to hearing her testimony.

Finally, let me close by emphasizing the importance of elevating the issue of women's issues globally, the question of sexual violence, violence against women, in general, to the international arena. I call on my colleagues in Congress to pass the International Violence Against Women's Act that Senator Boxer and I introduced last week. I believe the world is watching and the time is now.

My thanks to you, Mr. Chairman, to Senator Flake and to our witnesses. I look forward to hearing their testimony.

Senator COONS. Thank you very much, Chairman Menendez.

And we all look forward to the testimony of our witnesses today.

I would like to welcome our first panel. Ambassador Robert Jackson, Principal Deputy Assistant Secretary of State for African Affairs; Earl Gast, Assistant Administrator of Africa at USAID; and Ms. Alice Friend, a Principal Director for African Affairs at the Department of Defense—make up our first panel.

And our second panel will be Lantana Abdullahi, project manager for Search for Common Ground, who is currently watching this hearing and will be joining us later via Google Hangout, from Jos, Nigeria. We look forward to Ms. Abdullahi's testimony, commend her courage, and are honored by the opportunity to hear a voice from northern Nigeria today.

I want to thank our first-panel witnesses for being here today, and welcome your opening statements.

STATEMENT OF HON. ROBERT P. JACKSON, PRINCIPAL DEPUTY ASSISTANT SECRETARY OF STATE FOR AFRICAN AFFAIRS, U.S. DEPARTMENT OF STATE, WASHINGTON, DC

Ambassador JACKSON. Chairman Coons, Ranking Member Flake, Chairman Menendez, other members of the committee, thank you for inviting me to update you about U.S. efforts to address the chilling threat that Boko Haram represents to Nigeria, one of our most important partners in sub-Saharan Africa. Assistant Secretary for African Affairs Thomas Greenfield regrets that her travel schedule prevented her from being here today. However, she will be attending the Regional Summit organized by French President Hollande in Paris on Saturday.

It has now been 1 month since Boko Haram kidnapped the 200 young women from the town of Chibok in northeastern Nigeria. At the time of the kidnapping, these brave young women had returned to their high school in order to complete examinations that would allow them to attend university. By seeking knowledge and opportunity, they represented a challenge to Boko Haram, since it opposes democracy and formal education. Indeed, Boko Haram has attempted to crush the kind of faith in the promise of education and prosperity that families in Chibok showed.

The attack is part of a long, terrible trend. Boko Haram fighters have repeatedly targeted schools. In February, Boko Haram massacred at least 29 people when it destroyed a rural boarding school in Adamawa. Boko Haram has murdered police officers, snatched children, destroyed churches, burned schools, attacked mosques, driven people from their homes, challenged the government's authority, and kidnapped Westerners in both Nigeria and neighboring Cameroon.

Since January 1, Boko Haram has killed over 1,000 people, making Nigeria's struggle against this group one of the deadliest conflicts in Africa today. In addition to terrorizing the capital and other cities, Boko Haram attacks villages and military installations. The abductions in Chibok fit into a larger pattern of violence. Throughout northeastern Nigeria, teachers and students have learned to fear the gunmen who come in the night to kill young men and teachers and steal away young women. Some of the young women from Chibok daringly escaped their captors, but many more remained prisoners of Boko Haram's leaders, Abubakar Shekau, and his brutal followers.

We join the world, the people of Nigeria, and the parents of these children, in expressing our outrage of Boko Haram's shocking acts and its perverse ideology. This tragic kidnapping calls us to redouble our efforts to defeat a malicious terrorist organization that has troubled Nigeria for more than a decade. World leaders, including President Obama, have pledged their full support to the government and people of Nigeria as they seek to safely recover and assist these courageous young women.

We acted swiftly to carry out the President's pledge. By Monday, May 12, we had deployed an 18-member interagency team to advise the Nigerian Government as it works to bring back the young women—specifically, by advising on how to safely recover and assist these girls, offering specialized expertise on military and law enforcement best practices, hostage negotiation, intelligence-gathering, strategic communications, and how to mitigate the risk of future kidnappings. USAID has mobilized resources to provide humanitarian assistance to those affected by Boko Haram violence, including through the provision of psychosocial and medical support and treatment. We are cooperating fully with our partners— the U.K., France, and a host of other countries—who are also dedicating significant interagency manpower, resources, and time to this effort.

Mr. Chairman, a peaceful and stable Nigeria is crucially important to the future of Africa, and we cannot stay on the sidelines if it stumbles. Nigeria has the largest economy and largest population. We look to Nigeria as an ally in our quest to help Africans lead lives free of violence and filled with possibility. As an engine of growth and a political giant, Nigeria is vital to the success of President Obama's 2012 strategy toward sub-Saharan Africa. As we implement the strategy, we are focusing on building democratic, prosperous, and secure Nigeria.

Since Boko Haram came to the world's attention with a massive uprising in 2009, we have been working to help Nigeria counter this threat. We provide Nigeria with security assistance, which goes toward professionalizing the Nigerian military, investigating bomb sites, and enhancing border security. We have increasingly placed our response to Boko Haram in a regional context. Through our Trans-Saharan Counterterrorism Partnership, the Global Counterterrorism Forum, and our bilateral relationships with Nigeria's neighbors, we are encouraging greater information-sharing and border security efforts.

The importance of regional coordination is clear at a time like this as Nigeria and its partners seek to prevent Boko Haram from smuggling young women across the border or using neighboring countries as safe havens. I must note, however, that our ability to encourage regional collaboration is made more difficult at this time, as our highly qualified nominees to be the Ambassadors to Niger and Cameroon continue to await confirmation by the full Senate.

We have also joined the international effort to isolate Boko Haram. In June 2012, the State Department designated Boko Haram's top commanders as specially designated global terrorists. In June 2013, the State Department added Abubakar Shekau, Boko Haram's leader, to our Rewards for Justice Program and offered up to $7 million for information leading to his location. In November 2013, the State Department designated Boko Haram and Ansaru as foreign terrorist organizations. And last week, our Ambassador met President Jonathan, and they agreed on the importance of quick action on the U.N. designation of Boko Haram as a terrorist group. This week, Nigeria brought this question to the U.N. Security Council.

At the same time, we have been urging Nigeria to reform its approach to Boko Haram. From our own difficult experiences in

Afghanistan and Iraq, we know that turning the tide of an insurgency requires more than force. The state must demonstrate to its citizens that it can protect them and offer them opportunity. When soldiers destroy towns, kill civilians, and detain innocent people with impunity, mistrust takes root. We share these lessons with our partners in Nigeria, urging them to ensure that security services respect human rights and officials end a culture of impunity while people see the benefits of government and diverse voices are heard and represented in the capital.

We have seen some signs of reform. National Security Advisor Sambo Dasuki's March announcement of a soft approach to countering violent extremism was encouraging. And we have worked through our Counterterrorism and Conflict Stabilization Operations Bureaus to promote narratives of nonviolence in Nigeria.

As we strike a balance between counseling and empowering Nigeria, we regularly send high-level diplomats to Nigeria. On May 12 and 13, our Under Secretary for Civilian Security, Democracy, and Human Rights, Dr. Sarah Sewall, and AFRICOM commander, General David Rodriguez, were in Nigeria to discuss how to intensify our efforts against Boko Haram, reform human rights practices, and pursue a comprehensive approach.

All of these policy tools—our security assistance, our legal and sanctions actions, and our diplomatic engagement—constitute the framework within which we are working to help Nigeria bring back these girls kidnapped by Boko Haram. Resolving this crisis is now one of the highest priorities of the U.S. Government.

Nevertheless, Nigeria's conflict with Boko Haram will not end when these young women are brought home. Consequently, throughout this crisis, our assistance is framed by our broader and long-term policy goal of helping the Nigerians implement a comprehensive response to defeat Boko Haram that protects civilians, respects human rights, and addresses the underlying causes of conflict. We are sharing with the Government of Nigeria practices and strategies that will bolster its future efforts to defeat this deadly movement.

Nigeria's importance and the violent attacks committed by Boko Haram are both growing. We cannot ignore either trend. We welcome the committee's interest in these urgent matters, and we look forward to continuing to work with you as we strive to bring these young women home and to address the broader threat.

I look forward to your questions. Thank you.

[The prepared statement of Ambassador Jackson follows:]

PREPARED STATEMENT OF AMBASSADOR ROBERT P. JACKSON

Chairman Coons, Ranking Member Flake, and members of the committee, thank you for inviting me to update you about U.S. efforts to address the chilling threat that Boko Haram represents to Nigeria, one of our most important partners in sub-Saharan Africa.

It has now been 1 month since Boko Haram kidnapped more than 200 hundred girls from the town of Chibok in northeastern Nigeria. At the time of the kidnapping, these brave girls had returned to their high school in order to complete examinations that would allow them to attend university. By seeking knowledge and opportunity, they represented a challenge to Boko Haram in the heart of its area of operations. As the world now knows, Boko Haram opposes democracy and formal education. It has attempted to crush the kind of faith in the promise of education and prosperity that families in Chibok showed.

Boko Haram, the terrorist organization that kidnapped these girls, has shown it has no regard for human life. It has been killing innocent people in Nigeria for some time, and the attack at Chibok is part of that long, terrible trend. This year alone, Boko Haram has murdered more than 1,000 innocent people in vicious attacks on schools, churches, and mosques. Since 2013, it has targeted and systematically kidnapped women—including these girls—seeking to deny them the education and opportunity they deserve. The abductions in Chibok fit into this larger pattern of violence. Throughout northeastern Nigeria, innocent civilians are terrified by gunmen who come in the night to kill young men and teachers and steal away young women.

Boko Haram has also retained its ability to target Abuja, as we saw with two recent bombings at the Nyanya bus depot outside the capital. And we're concerned by the expansion of the group's operations beyond Nigeria, including in Cameroon where it has also conducted kidnappings. The group is not just a Nigerian problem; it is a regional security problem.

We join the world, the people of Nigeria, and the parents of these children in expressing our outrage at Boko Haram's shocking acts and its perverse ideology.

Young people, in Nigeria and across the globe, deserve the chance to pursue their dreams without suffering the predations of violent extremists. What happened in Nigeria resonates around the world, and pleas to free the kidnapped schoolgirls have come from First Lady Michelle Obama, from Pakistani activist Malala Yousafzai, U.N. Special Envoy for Global Education Gordon Brown, and other champions of women's right to an education.

This tragic kidnapping demands that we redouble our efforts to defeat a Foreign Terrorist Organization that has troubled Nigeria for more than a decade. World leaders, including President Obama, have pledged their full support to the government and people of Nigeria as they seek the safe return of these brave girls. We acted swiftly to carry out the President's pledge. By Monday, May 12, the U.S. Government had deployed an 18-member interagency team to provide military and law enforcement assistance, as well as intelligence, surveillance, and reconnaissance support. We have provided commercial imagery and are flying manned and unmanned ISR aircraft over Nigeria to support the search. We are working closely with international partners on the ground, including the U.K. and France, and we are pressing for additional multilateral action, including U.N. Security Council sanctions on Boko Haram. As the President has directed, we will do everything possible to support the Nigerians in their efforts to find and free these girls. But we won't stop there. We can and must continue to work closely with Nigeria to prevent Boko Haram from harming any more innocent people.

Given Nigeria's importance, Boko Haram cannot be allowed to continue its array of bloody tactics: murdering police officers, snatching children, destroying churches, burning schools, attacking mosques, driving people from their homes, and challenging the government's authority.

Mr. Chairman, a peaceful and stable Nigeria is crucially important to the future of Africa, and we cannot stay on the sidelines if it stumbles. Nigeria has the continent's largest population and biggest economy. We look to Nigeria as a partner in our quest to help Africans lead lives free of violence and filled with possibility. As an engine of growth, a fountainhead of art and industry, and a political giant, Nigeria is vital to the success of President Obama's 2012 Strategy Toward Sub-Saharan Africa. As we implement that strategy, we are focusing on building a democratic, prosperous, and secure Nigeria.

Since Boko Haram came to the world's attention with a massive uprising in 2009, we have been working to help Nigeria counter this threat. We provide Nigeria with security cooperation, which goes toward professionalizing the Nigerian military, investigating bomb sites, improving border security, and carrying out responsible counterterrorism operations. As we hear reports of Boko Haram cells in neighboring countries, we have increasingly placed our response to Boko Haram in a regional context. Through our Trans-Sahara Counterterrorism Partnership, the Global Counterterrorism Forum, and our bilateral relationships with Nigeria's neighbors, we are encouraging greater information-sharing and border security efforts.

At the same time, we have been urging Nigeria to reform its approach to Boko Haram. From our own difficult experiences in Afghanistan and Iraq, we know that turning the tide of an insurgency requires more than force. The state must demonstrate to its citizens that it can protect them and offer them opportunity. When soldiers destroy towns, kill civilians, and detain innocent people with impunity, mistrust takes root. When governments neglect the economic development of remote areas, confidence can falter. We share these lessons with our partners in Nigeria, urging them to ensure that security services respect human rights; officials end a culture of impunity; people see the benefits of government; and diverse voices are heard and represented in the capital. We have seen some signs of reform—we were encouraged in March of this year to see National Security Advisor Sambo Dasuki announce his ''soft approach'' to countering violent extremism, though Nigeria needs to follow through on implementing this strategy. We have also worked through our Counterterrorism and Conflict and Stabilization Operations Bureaus to promote narratives of nonviolence in Nigeria, and we are working broadly to protect civilians, prevent atrocities, and ensure respect for human rights.

At the same time, we are providing law enforcement assistance, including by training Nigerian law enforcement officials on basic forensics, hostage negotiations, leadership, and task force development.

To counter the spread of violent extremist ideology, we support programs and initiatives—including job training and education—that create economic alternatives for those vulnerable to being recruited by terrorist organizations.

All of this is part of a coordinated effort to help strengthen Nigeria's ability to respond responsibly and effectively to these challenges in a way that ensures civilians are protected and human rights are respected.

We have also joined the international effort to isolate Boko Haram. In June 2012, the State Department designated Boko Haram's top commanders as Specially Designated Global Terrorists under section 1(b) of Executive Order 13224. In June 2013, the State Department added Abubakar Shekau, Boko Haram's official leader, to our Rewards for Justice Program and offered up to $7 million for information leading to his location. In November 2013, the State Department designated Boko Haram and Ansaru as Foreign Terrorist Organizations, under Section 219 of the Immigration and Nationality Act, as amended, and as Specially Designated Global Terrorists under section 1(b) of Executive Order 13224. Last week, our Ambassador met President Jonathan on the margins of the World Economic Forum, and they agreed on the importance of quick action on the U.N. designation of Boko Haram as a terrorist group. The United Nations Security Council has renewed calls for regional cooperation to address Boko Haram. This week, Nigeria brought this question to the U.N. Security Council. And as I mentioned, we continue to work with Nigeria and others to press for U.N. Security Council sanctions on Boko Haram.

The importance of regional and multilateral coordination is clear at a time like this, as Nigeria and its partners seek to prevent Boko Haram from smuggling young women across the border or using neighboring countries as safe havens. I must note, however, that our ability to encourage regional collaboration is made more difficult, at this time, as our highly qualified nominees to be the U.S. Ambassadors to Niger and Cameroon continue to await confirmation by the full Senate.

As we strike a balance between helping empower Nigeria and counseling its government on reform, we engage regularly with Nigeria at all levels of our government. President Obama and Nigerian President Jonathan discussed security issues during their bilateral meeting on the margins of the U.N. General Assembly last September. Most recently, our Under Secretary for Civilian Security, Democracy, and Human Rights, Dr. Sarah Sewall, and U.S. Africa Command Commander General David Rodriguez spent May 12 and 13 in Nigeria. They met senior Nigerian security officials to discuss how to intensify efforts against Boko Haram, reform human rights practices, and pursue a comprehensive approach to Boko Haram. Under Secretary Sewall and General Rodriguez devoted considerable attention to the crisis surrounding the kidnapped women. Under Secretary Sewall called the principal of the young women's school in Chibok to express U.S. outrage and deep concern about the deplorable kidnapping.

All of these policy tools—our security cooperation, our legal and sanctions actions, and our diplomatic engagement—constitute the framework within which we are working to help Nigeria safely bring back the women kidnapped by Boko Haram. Resolving this crisis is now one of the highest priorities of the U.S. Government. As I mentioned when I began, we deployed an interagency team to advise Nigerian authorities on how to recover safely and assist these young women. Led by a senior diplomat from our Africa Bureau, the team is liaising with counterparts across Nigeria's Government to offer specialized expertise on military and law enforcement best practices, hostage negotiation, intelligence gathering, strategic communications, and how to mitigate the risks of future kidnappings. At the same time, USAID has mobilized resources to provide humanitarian assistance to those affected by Boko Haram violence, including through the provision of psychosocial and medical support and treatment. We are cooperating thoroughly with the U.K., France, and a host of other countries who are also dedicating significant interagency manpower, resources, and time to this effort. Our field team remains in close, coordinated contact with State Department headquarters here in Washington.

Nevertheless, Nigeria's conflict with Boko Haram will not end when these young women are bought home. Consequently, throughout this crisis, our assistance is framed by our broader and long-term policy goal of helping the Nigerians implement a comprehensive response to defeating Boko Haram that protects civilians, respects human rights, and addresses the underlying causes of the conflict. We are sharing practices and strategies with the Government of Nigeria that will bolster its future efforts to defeat this deadly movement.

Nigeria's importance and the violent attacks committed by Boko Haram are both growing. We cannot ignore either trend. We welcome your interest in these urgent matters, and we look forward to continuing to work with you as we strive to bring these young women home and address the broader threat posed by Boko Haram.

Senator COONS. Thank you, Ambassador Jackson.
Assistant Administrator Gast.

STATEMENT OF HON. EARL GAST, ASSISTANT ADMINISTRA-TOR FOR AFRICAN AFFAIRS, U.S. AGENCY FOR INTERNA-TIONAL DEVELOPMENT, WASHINGTON, DC

Mr. GAST. Chairman Coons, Ranking Member Flake, and Chairman Menendez, thank you for the opportunity for me to speak before you today about the brutal kidnapping of more than 250 young girls from their school just 1 month ago.

This latest brutality was not an isolated incident. For years, Boko Haram has terrorized the people of northern Nigeria. They have attempted to exploit northern Nigeria's low level of infrastructure, development, and security that affects all aspects of life, from economic growth to access to basic services, resulting in the north's growing isolation.

This conflict has caused decreases in agricultural production, price spikes, and serious concerns about food security, both in the north and also in neighboring states. For example, Niger is import-dependent and dependent on exports from Nigeria.

In Nigeria, nearly 4.2 million persons are at risk of food insecurity, and continued unrest will likely have long-term impacts on nutrition, agriculture, and trade. It is projected that by 2015 Nigeria will soon be home to the largest number of persons worldwide living in extreme poverty.

In May 2013, due to an escalation of violence, the Government of Nigeria declared a state of emergency in Adamawa, Borno, and Yobe states. In early 2014, attacks carried out by Boko Haram militants killed more than 1,500 persons. According to the U.N., violence had displaced more than a quarter of a million persons to neighboring states by only a few months later, in March, 70 percent of whom were women and children. In communities hosting internally displaced persons, the presence of additional families is straining local resources, including already stretched water systems and basic commodities.

To determine the extent of this crisis, the U.N., along with key international NGOs, are currently conducting a multiagency, multisector needs assessment, and USAID is a part of that assessment team. Last week, a team of humanitarian professionals from the U.N. and the NGO community traveled to the areas that are now part of the state of emergency, as well as three bordering states that have received most of the IDPs, the internally displaced persons. This team is meeting with state and local officials, with the displaced persons themselves, and other community members to establish the number of displaced persons, where they are living, their ability to access food, income, health care, education, and water and hygiene. The team will also evaluate food security, nutrition, and protection services along with identifying actors who are on the ground and who can help develop the most effective approaches to deliver relief.

We will use the results of this mission to shape the provision of humanitarian assistance, in partnership with others, to meet urgent humanitarian needs among affected families. Assistance will include food, shelter, safe drinking water, emergency treatment of acute malnutrition, community-based psychosocial support, and programs target at preventing and treating sexual and gender-based violence.

Exacerbating this humanitarian crisis is Boko Haram's assaults on youth seeking education. A good education is a global public good, and it is a necessary ingredient for economic development and poverty reduction. Education enables people to live healthier lives, fulfill their potential, and it also contributes to open, inclusive, and vibrant societies. These attacks undermine northern Nigeria's already precarious educational system by destroying schools, forcing others to close, and keeping thousands of students and teachers out of the classroom. School attendance in the region, already well below the national rate, will continue to suffer.

USAID has active programs in nearly all of Nigeria's northern states, with a particular focus on Bauchi and Sokoto. Through our education programs in the north, we have increased access to basic education services for more than 15,000 orphans and vulnerable children; we have strengthened the capacity of some 24 education-related NGOs; and we have also influenced Nigeria's Educational Research and Development Council to include reading as a core objective of its curriculum.

USAID's conflict mitigation program, active in six states in the north, including Borno, the state most affected by the violence, has funded numerous community training programs on conflict mitigation. We have supported and trained conflict management and mitigation councils. And we have carried out, in partnership with local organizations, phone-in interfaith dialogues on radio and television programs.

Today, our thoughts are with the schoolgirls and their families and the millions of Nigerians forced to live under the threat of Boko Haram's violence every day.

Thank you. And I look forward to your questions.

[The prepared statement of Mr. Gast follows:]

PREPARED STATEMENT OF HON. EARL GAST

USAID partners around the world to end extreme poverty and promote resilient, democratic societies, while advancing our security and prosperity. Our work in northern Nigeria highlights the nexus between security, stability, and poverty reduction. We are committed to working with Nigeria to build a peaceful society that promotes inclusive economic growth and lifts its citizens out of poverty.

One month ago, Boko Haram militants kidnapped more than 250 young girls from their school in an attack so shocking it mobilized the world behind returning these girls to their families. But this latest brutality was not an isolated incident. For years, Boko Haram has terrorized the people of northern Nigeria through bombings, kidnapping, and sexual violence.

For decades, development in the northern part of the country has markedly lagged behind the relative progress made in the south as is evident through comparison of development indicators in Nigeria's six geopolitical zones. In the three northern zones, per capita incomes are significantly lower than the national average. Literacy in the southwest zone is around 80 percent for girls, while in the northeast it is only 15 percent. Health statistics paint a similar picture of disparity. Immunization coverage in the northeast is only about 8 percent, while in the south-south it is closer to 36 percent.

In recent years, Boko Haram has attempted to exploit northern Nigeria's low level of infrastructure, public services, and security. Boko Haram attacks have affected all aspects of life, from economic growth to access to basic services, and resulted in the north's growing isolation. Commercial activity in Kano, once a national economic hub, is estimated to have decreased by 50 percent in recent years, due in large part to the stream of businesses that have left northern states like Borno and Kaduna for the stability of the south.

The conflict has caused decreases in agricultural production, price spikes, and serious concerns about food security both in the north and neighboring states, particularly import-dependent Niger. In Nigeria, nearly 4.2 million people are at risk of food insecurity, and continued unrest will likely have long-term impacts on nutrition, agriculture, and trade.

Access to health care has dramatically declined in the hardest hit conflict areas; in Borno state, doctors are fleeing and clinics are closing, forcing the population into neighboring Cameroon for basic health services. Boko Haram has also been targeting cell phone towers so people in the region have less access to communications.

As violence began to escalate, the Government of Nigeria declared a state of emergency in Adamawa, Borno, and Yobe states in May 2013. In early 2014, attacks carried out by Boko Haram militants killed more than 1,500 people. According to the U.N., violence had displaced more than a quarter million people to neighboring states by March 2014—70 percent of them women and children. An additional 61,000 people, including returning migrants, have also fled to neighboring Niger, Cameroon, and Chad, where they are living in host communities.

In communities hosting internally displaced persons, the presence of additional families is straining local resources, including already-stretched water systems and basic commodities. Increasing numbers of female-headed households is forcing widows to become the sole providers for their families. Such households and widows are exposed to additional violence within host communities. In the absence of their husbands, widows also lack access to financial resources, exacerbated by inheritance laws, and systems that limit women's ownership of property.

SITUATIONAL ASSESSMENT

Due to insecurity, presence of aid workers in the most affected areas is very limited and we do not yet have a comprehensive picture of the overall humanitarian situation. To determine the extent of the crisis, the U.N. along with key international nongovernmental organizations are currently conducting a multiagency, multisector needs assessment. Last week, a team of humanitarian professionals from the U.N. and NGOs traveled to the areas in states of emergency (Borno, Yobe, and Adamawa) as well as three bordering states (Bauchi, Gombe, and Taraba) that have received the most internally displaced people.

This team is currently interviewing state and local officials and meeting with internally displaced persons and other community members to establish the number of displaced people, where they live, and their level of access to food, income, health care, education, water, sanitation, and hygiene. The team will also evaluate food security, nutrition, and protection services, identify humanitarian actors still on the ground, and develop the most effective approaches to deliver relief and identify opportunities to strengthen the capacity of state governments and local partners to monitor displacement, report, assess, and coordinate delivery of relief.

USAID humanitarian experts have been involved in the assessment process since the beginning, working to help define indicators and processes. USAID humanitarian experts are currently in Nigeria and will continue to support the work of the U.N. and other agencies. USAID will use the results of this mission to shape the provision of humanitarian assistance in partnership with implementing organizations to meet urgent humanitarian needs among affected families. Assistance may include providing food, shelter, and household items for displaced populations; safe water in communities whose resources have been overstretched because of an influx of new families; support to emergency treatment of acute malnutrition; or community-based psychosocial support and programs targeted at the prevention and treatment of sexual and gender-based violence. USAID is also exploring opportunities for collaboration with key Nigerian agencies, the Nigerian National Emergency Management Agency, local emergency response actors as well as supporting efforts to increase food security data collection and analysis to inform potential response options.

Once completed, the U.N. and USAID assessments will give us a better understating of the situation and how best to respond, taking into account the operational realities of programming in Northern Nigeria.

AN ATTACK ON EDUCATION

Exacerbating the humanitarian crisis, Boko Haram's assaults on youth seeking education has become ever more brazen over the past 2 years. A good education is a global public good, and a necessary ingredient for economic development and poverty reduction. Education enables people to live healthier and more productive lives, allowing them to fulfill their own potential, as well as to strengthen and contribute to open, inclusive and economically vibrant societies.

Boko Haram's attacks on schools had consisted of destroying empty school buildings at night, but more recently has shifted to targeting Muslim and non-Muslim students and staff with guns, knives, and explosives. The group has killed or wounded hundreds of students and teachers since June 2013. The mass abduction of female students in Chibok marked a frightening shift: While in prior attacks, Boko Haram generally instructed female students to flee, they are now publically calling on girls to abandon Western education or be taken as slaves.

Boko Haram is also seeking to perpetuate child marriage as an acceptable practice and is using it to sow fear, intimidation, and coercion.

These attacks undermine northern Nigeria's already precarious educational system by destroying schools, forcing others to close, and keeping thousands of students and teachers out of the classroom. School attendance in the region, already well below the national rate, most likely will continue to suffer.

USAID ASSISTANCE

USAID has active programs in nearly all of Nigeria's northern states, with a particular focus on Bauchi and Sokoto. Through our education programs in the north, we have increased access to basic education services for over 15,000 orphans and vulnerable children, strengthened the capacity of 24 education-related nongovernmental organizations to responsibly manage their finances, and influenced Nigeria's Educational Research and Development Council to include reading as a part of the education curriculum.

Through our economic growth programs, USAID has built the capacity of export firms, helped medium-sized, small, and microenterprises gain access to loans, and supported the development of a new customs and excise management act to reform and modernize the Nigerian customs service. At the same time, the Feed the Future program has helped Nigerian farmers more than double their yields in maize, rice, and sorghum, and leveraged millions of dollars in credit for thousands of beneficiaries and for numerous private sector partnerships.

USAID has also helped the Sokoto and Bauchi State Houses of Assembly pass public procurement and fiscal responsibility laws, trained over 900 government officials in public procurement and financial management practices, and assisted with the passing of the federal freedom of information act and its adoption at the state levels.

USAID's conflict mitigation program—active in six states in the north, including Borno, the state most affected state by Boko Haram's violence—has funded numerous community training programs on conflict mitigation, reconstituted and trained Conflict Management and Mitigation Regional Councils, and carried out phone-in interfaith dialogues on radio and television programs.

Regionally, the Trans-Sahara Counterterrorism Partnership, which USAID implements alongside the Departments of State and Defense, includes a regional Peace for Development program in Burkina Faso, Niger, and Chad—areas that are vulnerable as they may become fertile ground for the expansion of violent extremist groups. This initiative applies a holistic, community-led approach that has reached nearly 3.8 million people from at-risk groups through youth-led community mobilization activities, radio programming, and training in management skills, budgeting, leadership, vocational trades, and conflict resolution. In other areas of the Sahel, USAID supports a vocational education program in Mauritania and has expanded our program to counter violent extremism to key areas of Northern Mali. Given the immense size of the Sahel, interventions are limited to communities with the highest risk factors, which have been identified through assessments conducted by the project. A number of those target communities are in areas of Niger and Chad that border Nigeria. These programs have led to a noticeable rise in community action. This week, a local youth organization in Bamako, Mali, is sponsoring a mass demonstration and public outreach around the issue of the kidnapping of the Nigerian schoolgirls.

Today our thoughts are with the schoolgirls, their families; and the millions of Nigerians forced to live under the threat of Boko Haram's violence every day.

Senator COONS. Thank you very much.

Principal Director Friend, thank you for joining us today. We welcome your testimony.

STATEMENT OF ALICE FRIEND, PRINCIPAL DIRECTOR FOR AFRICAN AFFAIRS, U.S. DEPARTMENT OF DEFENSE, WASHINGTON, DC

Ms. FRIEND. Chairman Coons, Ranking Member Flake, members of the committee, thank you for calling us together to address the deeply disturbing abductions of over 270 schoolgirls in northern Nigeria by the terrorist organization Boko Haram.

People of good will across the globe have been horrified by this barbarous act and are rightly demanding that the Nigerian authorities take immediate measures to recover the girls, and are asking what those of us in the international community can do to support Nigerian efforts.

Last Friday, the United States dispatched a multidisciplinary State Department-led team of experts to Abuja to provide the Government of Nigeria with the specialized advice and expertise it needs to respond to these abductions. DOD has provided four subject-matter experts from U.S. Africa Command Headquarters in Stuttgart, Germany, to augment 10 DOD personnel already assigned to our Embassy in Abuja as part of this interagency team. In addition, two military officers with extensive experience supporting the Counter-Lord's Resistance Army Mission in Uganda also have been temporarily relocated to Abuja to provide their advice and assistance.

In total, 16 DOD personnel with medical, intelligence, counterterrorism, and communications expertise have been assigned exclusively to the mission of advising the Nigerian security forces' efforts to recover these girls. Secretary Jackson also mentioned the concurrent visit of the commander of Africa Command, General Rodriguez, to engage with his Nigerian counterparts alongside Under Secretary Sewall. Their initial efforts have been to work with Nigerian security personnel to analyze Nigerian operations, identify gaps and shortfalls, and otherwise provide requested expertise and information to the Nigerian authorities, including through the use of intelligence, surveillance, and reconnaissance support. We are also working closely with other international partners, including the U.K. and France, to coordinate multilateral actions and maximize our collective assistance efforts.

Mr. Chairman, the threat to Nigeria from Boko Haram has grown over the past 5 years, and mutates day by day, extending its reach, increasing the sophistication and lethality of its attacks, and growing its military capacity. These most recent attacks are especially unconscionable because they were perpetrated against innocent girls and because of the sheer scale of the attack in Chibok.

Unfortunately, these kidnappings are only the most recent outrages in a growing portfolio of attacks perpetrated by Boko Haram in its war against education. On July 6, 2013, in an attack on the secondary school in Mamudo Village, 29 students were killed, including reports that some were burned alive when their dormitory was deliberately set on fire. Overnight between September 28 and 29, 2013, upward of 40 students were slaughtered in a nighttime attack on the Yobe State College of Agriculture. And in yet another nighttime attack, this at the Buni Yadi Federal Government College in February of this year, at least 59 people, including boys ranging in age from 11 to 18, were killed.

The Department has been deeply concerned for some time by how much the Government of Nigeria has struggled to keep pace with Boko Haram's growing lethality and capabilities. Recognizing this threat and the need for Nigeria to adopt a whole-of-government approach to defeating it, over the past several years DOD has undertaken a number of initiatives to assist Nigeria in its counter-Boko Haram efforts. For example, we have supported the establishment of counter-IED and civil-military operations capacity within the Nigerian Army. We have also supported the establishment of an intelligence fusion center in an effort to promote information-sharing among various national security entities and, overall, to enable more effective and responsible intelligence-driven counter-terrorism operations. More recently, we have begun working with Nigeria's newly created Ranger Battalion to impart the specialized skills and disciplines needed to mount effective counterterrorism operations.

Mr. Chairman, as dedicated as the Department of Defense is to supporting Nigeria in its fight against Boko Haram and in recovering these girls safely, we cannot ignore that Nigeria can be an extremely challenging partner to work with. In the face of this sophisticated threat, Nigeria's security forces have been slow to adapt with new strategies, new doctrines, and new tactics. Even more troubling, Nigeria's record of atrocities perpetrated by some of its security forces during operations against Boko Haram have been widely documented. As we have advised the Nigerians, consistent with U.S. law and policy, we review security-force units who may receive assistance, and we cannot, and do not, provide assistance when we have credible information that those units have committed gross violations of human rights.

With this important consideration in mind, we have worked to engage where and how we are able to in viewing our engagements and training efforts with human rights and Law of Armed Conflict modules and emphasizing the importance of the broad counter-insurgency approach that we, ourselves, have spent so much blood and treasure fulfilling. Indeed, if this tragic episode is to end the way we all hope it will, Nigeria's leaders must continue to match their public statements with a serious and focused response that draws on all elements of their government and makes maximum use of the resources international partners are offering to them. This will not be an easy task. We are still seeking information on whether, where, and how the girls may have been dispersed. But, DOD is committed to supporting Nigeria in locating these girls and seeing them safely returned to their loved ones.

Thank you again for convening us here today, and I look forward to your questions.

[The prepared statement of Ms. Friend follows:]

Chairman Coons, Ranking Member Flake, members of the subcommittee, thank you for calling us together to address the deeply disturbing recent abductions of over 270 school girls in northern Nigeria by the terrorist organization Boko Haram. People of good will across the globe have been horrified by this barbarous act and are rightly demanding that the Nigerian authorities take immediate measures to recover the girls and are asking what those of us in the international community can do to support Nigerian efforts.

Last Friday, the United States dispatched a multidisciplinary, State Department-led team of experts to Abuja to provide the Government of Nigeria with the specialized advice and expertise it needs to respond to these abductions. DOD has provided four subject matter experts from USAFRICOM headquarters to augment 10 DOD personnel already assigned to our Embassy in Abuja as part of this interagency team. In addition, two military officers with extensive experience supporting the counter-Lord's Resistance Army mission in Uganda also have been temporarily relocated to Abuja to provide advice and assistance. In total, 16 DOD personnel with medical, intelligence, counterterrorism and communications expertise have been assigned exclusively to the mission of advising the Nigerian security forces' efforts to recover these girls safely. Their initial efforts have been to work with Nigerian security personnel to analyze Nigerian operations, identify gaps and shortfalls, and otherwise provide requested expertise and information to the Nigerian authorities, including through the use of intelligence, surveillance, and reconnaissance support. We are also working closely with other international partners, including the U.K. and France, to coordinate multilateral actions and maximize our collective assistance efforts.

Our intent is to support Nigerian-led efforts to recover the girls and help catalyze greater efforts to secure the Nigerian population from the menace of Boko Haram. The Department of Defense stands ready to do what we can to help the Nigerian Government, but both the immediate and the long-term solutions to the threat Boko Haram poses to the people of Nigeria must be implemented by the Government of Nigeria if a sustained security is ever to be reached.

Mr. Chairman, that threat to Nigeria from Boko Haram has grown over the past 5 years and mutates day by day, extending its reach, increasing the sophistication and lethality of its attacks, and growing its military capacity. It has now proven on multiple occasions—for example, through its successful attack on a Nigerian air base in which two of the Nigerian air force's helicopters were destroyed, as well as the coordinated, methodical and highly successful attack at Giwa barracks—that it is now capable of directly and successfully engaging Nigeria's Armed Forces. Its expanded reach was also convincingly and tragically demonstrated when over 70 innocent Nigerian citizens were killed in a vehicle-borne IED attack just outside the national capital of Abuja.

These most recent attacks are especially unconscionable because they were perpetrated against innocent girls and because of the sheer scale of the attack in Chibok. Unfortunately these kidnappings are only the most recent outrages in a growing portfolio of attacks perpetrated by Boko Haram in its war against education. On June 16–17, 2013, seven students and two teachers were killed when Boko Haram members attacked the Government Secondary School in Damaturu, Yobe state. This was followed on July 6, 2013, by an attack on the secondary school in Mamudo village, in which 29 students were killed, including reports that some were burned alive when their dormitory was deliberately set on fire. On September 28–29, 2013, upward of 40 students were slaughtered in a nighttime attack by Boko Haram on the Yobe State College of Agriculture. And in yet another nighttime attack, this time at the Buni Yadi Federal Government College on February 18 of this year, at least 59 people, including boys ranging in age from 11 to 18, were killed.

The Department has been deeply concerned for some time by how much the Government of Nigeria has struggled to keep pace with Boko Haram's growing capabilities. Recognizing this threat and the need for Nigeria to adopt a whole-of-government approach to defeating it, over the past 2 years the United States has made a concerted effort to assist Nigeria in its counter-Boko Haram efforts. For its part, DOD has undertaken a number of initiatives. For example, we have supported the establishment of counter-IED and civil-military operations capacity within the Nigerian Army in order to make C–IED an integral part of Nigeria's security doctrine. The concept is to build Nigerian institutions so that C–IED skills are organic and can be maintained and passed along by the Nigerians themselves. We have also supported the establishment of an intelligence fusion center in an effort to promote information-sharing among various national security entities and, overall, to enable more effective and responsible intelligence-driven CT operations. More recently, we have begun working with Nigeria's newly created Ranger Battalion to impart the specialized skills and disciplines needed to mount effective CT operations.

As has been demonstrated during recent Boko Haram movements and attacks, porous borders with Nigeria's northeastern and western neighbors can also facilitate these terrorists' operations in the region. For this reason, DOD and the Department of State are working closely and actively to develop a regional response to the Boko Haram threat to enhance border security along Nigeria's common borders with Chad, Niger, and Cameroon. The concept is to build border security capacity with, and promote better cooperation and communication among, the security forces of each country. In some cases, assistance would go to the military, in others the gendarmerie, and in still others immigration forces, to more effectively detect and respond to the movement of Boko Haram members back and forth between Nigeria and its neighbors. If we can build these basic but critical capacities, serious progress can be made toward halting Boko Haram's spread and reversing some of the gains it has made.

As committed as the U.S. is to supporting Nigeria in its fight against Boko Haram and in returning these girls safely to their families, we cannot ignore that Nigeria can be an extremely challenging partner to work with. In general Nigeria has failed to mount an effective campaign against Boko Haram. In the face of a new and more sophisticated threat than it has faced before, its security forces have been slow to adapt with new strategies, new doctrines and new tactics. Even more troubling, Nigeria's record of atrocities perpetrated by some of its security forces during operations against Boko Haram has been widely documented. As we have advised the Nigerians, consistent with U.S. law and policy, we review security force units who may receive assistance, and we do not provide assistance when we have credible information that they have committed gross violations of human rights. With this important consideration in mind, we have worked to engage where and how we are able to, imbuing our engagements and training efforts with human rights and law of armed conflict modules and emphasizing the importance of the broad counterinsurgency approach that we ourselves spent so much blood and treasure fulfilling.

No discussion of how to address the Boko Haram threat would be complete without addressing some of the political dynamics in Nigeria underlying the security environment. In spite of its vast oil wealth, Nigeria continues to face enormous development challenges. These factors combine with pervasive federal and state government corruption and Boko Haram's brutal terrorization of the population have made northern Nigerians susceptible to antigovernment narratives and afforded the group a more permissive operating environment. The long-term solution to Boko Haram does not depend exclusively on Nigeria's military or security forces, but also requires Nigeria's national political leaders to give serious and sustained attention to addressing the systemic problems of corruption, the lack of effective and equitable governance, and the country's uneven social and economic development.

Nevertheless, we will not lose our focus on the heartrending event that has brought us here today. The tragic situation of these girls and the families who hope for their safe return has captured the attention of the world. As I have highlighted already, DOD is committed to supporting Nigeria's efforts to locate these girls and to seeing them safely returned to their loved ones. This will not be an easy task. We are still seeking information on whether and how the girls may have been dispersed. Indeed, if this tragic episode is to end the way we all hope it will, the government of Nigeria must continue to match its public statements with a serious and focused response that draws on all elements of its government and making maximum use of the resources international partners are making available to it.

Senator COONS. Thank you, Principal Director Friend.

Thank you, to this panel, for your testimony.

I would like to now begin questions in 7-minute rounds. And I will remind all of us, we have a scheduled vote at 11:15 and following a second-panel witness.

If I might start, I would just like to begin with a direct question to each of you. You have addressed this in longer form, but if I could just have a, in the interest of time, concise and direct answer. When did your agency make its first offer of assistance after the kidnappings? What did that offer entail? What was the Nigerian Government's response? And what do you see as the real impediments toward the Nigerians taking full advantage of the opportunities and resources we have offered?

Ambassador Jackson.

Ambassador JACKSON. Thank you, Mr. Chairman.

Secretary Kerry called President Jonathan roughly 2 weeks ago today, made the offer, which President Jonathan accepted with alacrity. And it involved intelligence collection and support and other resources that I described in my testimony.

Senator COONS. Assistant Administrator Gast.

Mr. GAST. Almost immediately after the incident, the Embassy and USAID declared a state of emergency, which allowed us to bring in additional resources and assessment teams. So, that was one way.

The second was, our Administrator almost immediately traveled—after the incident, traveled to Nigeria to meet with the government as well as participate in other discussions, but certainly did focus on this issue.

Senator COONS. Thank you.

Principal Director Friend.

Ms. FRIEND. Sir, the State Department took the lead in making the initial offers. However, once the Government of Nigeria, in fact, accepted our offer of assistance—I believe that was on the 4th of May—the Department had ISR overflight by the 9th of May.

Senator COONS. Thank you.

If I could, Ambassador Jackson—as you mentioned in your testimony, in 2012 the State Department deliberated over whether to designated Boko Haram as an organization—as a foreign terrorist organization—or to designate top leaders, which, indeed, happened in 2012, and then the group as a whole as an FTO the following year. But, what were the implications of designating those three individuals in 2012? And what additional steps have been taken by the administration to target Boko Haram's funding and other sources of support? And why was there not initially unanimity around designating the whole organization?

Ambassador JACKSON. Senator, the debate about whether to designate Boko Haram dates back many years, to at least 2011. And I think, as former Assistant Secretary Johnny Carson has explained in media interviews, the debate was really about the Nigerian attitude toward designation. The Government of Nigeria feared that designating these individuals and the organizations would bring them more attention, more publicity, and be counterproductive.

For some time, we accepted that point of view. And the fact that the Nigerians are only now asking the U.N. to designate them continues to reflect Nigerian hesitancy over the impact of these designations. But, we decided to move ahead in 2012, precisely because we were convinced that they met the criteria for designation.

Senator COONS. Thank you.

If you would, Assistant Administrator Gast, describe the strategy of the Nigerian Government to address the root causes of Boko Haram support in northern Nigeria. The hearing that we conducted 2 years ago could almost literally be repeated today, in terms of ongoing structural challenges that have led to this insurgency and have created the conditions, and sustained and, in some ways, accelerated the conditions, for Boko Haram.

Mr. GAST. As the Principal Deputy Assistant Secretary mentioned in his testimony, there is a realization within the national security—among the national security group, including the security advisor himself, Dasuki, that this is a major concern. And so, there are two units within the National Security Advisor's office that are working on developing plans for the north: one, a massive, long, multiyear development program; another one that would help address the immediate concerns of security, community, development. We are advising those two groups and helping identify areas where we can assist in providing programming support.

Senator COONS. Girls in Nigeria and around the world are risking their lives every day just to get an education. USAID does deliver significant support for education opportunities, and, in particular, for the inclusion of women and girls in education. But, with a decline in USAID's funding request for education programming, I am concerned we may not have enough resources to do what we should and what we must in Nigeria and elsewhere. USAID support is predominantly focused in Bauchi and Sokoto states—as you said, a small portion of the total north. Please speak, if you would, to the strategy for how to continue to support education, which really is the root cause of a lot of the violence, in this instance, the insistence on access to education for women.

Mr. GAST. Education has always been a robust element of our program support in Nigeria. And if one were to look at the continent as a whole, the budget for education in Nigeria represents about 10 percent of the entire education budget. So, it is a significant contribution that we are making.

The question is, Are we placing the resources in the right areas? And certainly because of access issues, it is extremely difficult to program resources in the north. We are working with DFID, the British development agency, and we believe we are very close to announcing a major effort to support education, primarily girls' education, secure education in the north.

Senator COONS. Thank you.

Principal Director Friend, tell me more, if you would, about the Trans-Sahel Counterterrorism Partnership and what we have done regionally with other countries that are directly affected by Boko Haram—Chad, Niger, Cameroon. And, if you would, just as a last question—you mentioned the gross human rights violations committed by some elements of the Nigerian Armed Forces. We are still able to find units with which we can partner. And it is still possible for the Nigerian military police and security forces to take the lead in ensuring the return—the safe return of the Nigerian schoolgirls. Is that not correct?

Ms. FRIEND. Yes, sir. I will take those questions in reverse. That is correct. I mentioned in my testimony the Ranger Battalion that we will begin training, in fact, this month, and pretraining programming has begun to lay in the groundwork for that. So, we are able to find units inside the Nigerian Armed Forces that, in fact, pass Leahy vetting, and have passed Leahy vetting. It is, however, a persistent and very troubling limitation on our ability to provide assistance, particularly training assistance, that the Nigerians so badly need. This is one of the things that we have been talking to them about for quite some time.

Another recent engagement that was also interagency in nature was a counterinsurgency-focused trip to Nigeria, I believe last fall, where we were urging them to take a more holistic approach, and a, frankly, much less brutal approach, in the north against Boko Haram.

To your question of the Trans-Sahel Counterterrorism Partnership, it is a State Department-led effort, so I do not want to speak out of turn for Mr. Jackson, but I will say that, in the region, we have been working increasingly with the Cameroonians and the Nigerians and the Chadians to talk about the regional threat that Boko Haram poses. As you, I am sure, have heard in the press, there is some thought that some of the girls may have been taken over international borders. And, of course, the border with Cameroon and Niger, in particular, is very porous, and we do know that Boko Haram does operate back and forth across the international border, particularly with Cameroon. The Cameroonian Government and the Cameroonian President, in particular, have recently been taking Boko Haram even more seriously than previously, and we are working with them and with the Nigerians and the Chadians to assist them and to do everything we can to ensure that all these countries coordinate with each other.

Senator COONS. Thank you very much.

Senator Flake.

Senator FLAKE. Thank you, Mr. Chairman.

Thanks for the testimony.

Ms. Friend, with our cooperation or assistance to the military, to what extent is it complicated by some of the rules and regulations we have about dealing with militaries that have human rights abuses lodged against them or have problems that way? What restrictions are we under? And how does that limit our ability to work with them?

Ms. FRIEND. So, essentially, sir, under the Leahy provision, any unit that we suspect of having committed gross human rights violations, we cannot provide military training or assistance to. The broader implications of your question, however—''How much does it affect our engagement with Nigeria?''—it affects it very much. We have struggled a great deal, in the past, to locate units that we can work with, and, indeed, to convince the Nigerians to change their tactics, techniques, and procedures toward Boko Haram.

Another way that we are very, very careful to ensure that we are only providing assistance to those who will not use it in ways that may affect civilians or otherwise violate international human rights standards is our intel-sharing. Though sharing intelligence with a foreign government that is available to—intelligence that is available to DOD would not normally be considered assistance subject to the DOD Leahy law, we nevertheless are exceedingly cautious when it comes to sharing information with the Nigerians, because of their unfortunate record. In this case, for example, we have sought assurances from them, that Ambassador Entwistle delivered a couple of days ago, that they will use any information that we pass to them from this ISR support in a manner consistent with international humanitarian and human rights law.

Senator FLAKE. As I understand it, we have a couple of issues with the military. One, they have been using pretty brutal tactics and pretty brutal justice, if you will, with regard to Boko Haram in the north, but also there is some fear that some of its ranks are infiltrated with Boko Haram sympathizers. Is that a concern, as well, the latter?

Ms. ABDULLAHI. That is a concern, sir. I would say an even greater concern is the incapacity of the Nigerian military and the Nigerian Government's failure to provide leadership to the military in a way that changes these tactics. The division in the north that mainly is engaging with Boko Haram, the 7th Division, has recently shown signs of real fear. They do not have the capabilities, the training, or the equipping that Boko Haram does. And Boko Haram is exceptionally brutal and indiscriminate in their attacks. And so, as heavyhanded as the forces on the Nigerian side have been, Boko Haram has been even more brutal.

And so, we are now looking at a military force that is, quite frankly, becoming afraid to even engage. And that is one of the things that we are talking to the military leadership in Abuja about right now, about how to get the training and also the orientation of the forces under control so that they will feel more competent to face the threat.

Senator FLAKE. The military's decline in effectiveness in Nigeria is really traced to fear that the political leadership has to military coup. And that has been the pattern that has been followed around other countries, as well. Is that what you trace the decline to? And is this political leadership now, this President and those around him, do they fear strengthening the military for that purpose, fearing a coup later? What is the relationship right now between the political leadership and the military?

Ms. FRIEND. The relationship between the political leadership and the military itself is reasonably healthy. My understanding is that the weakening of the Nigerian military does trace back a couple of decades, at least, to concerns about capability for a coup. At this point, that is not a concern in Nigeria.

Another concern, which my colleagues can also speak to, is that the Nigerian military has the same challenges with corruption that every other institution in Nigeria does. Much of the funding that goes to the Nigerian military is skimmed off the top, if you will.

Senator FLAKE. Assistant Administrator Gast, reports have been around for a while about kidnappings and whatnot in the north. Let me just read from one report. "For much of the past year, Boko Haram's fighters have stalked the rugged hills of northeastern Nigeria, forcing teenage boys into their trucks as recruits and snatching teenage girls as sex slaves," said Nigerian officials and analysts. "Villages and small towns in the northeast are dotted with parents who have not seen their children in months."

How aware has the State Department been of this activity? And should we have been more aware of the events that might have told us that a kidnapping of this kind was coming?

Mr. GAST. So, from AID's perspective—and I will let Deputy Assistant Secretary Jackson address it from State—yes, we are very aware. Access is an issue. And so, the programmatic response that we are able to deliver is less than it would be if we had access.

We do work with local organizations, and there are some very, very good local organizations that can help provide psychosocial services to families and to individuals, that can help promote dialogue between communities. Unfortunately, the capacity of them to expand and go into more areas and reach more deeply into pockets of society is somewhat limited.

Senator FLAKE. AID usually learns of these things just because of the programs that you do with the local population there. Mr. Jackson, can you speak from State's perspective? How aware were we of these kind of kidnappings and this activity going on long before the school kidnapping?

Ambassador JACKSON. Senator, we have been very aware. And, as Ambassador to Cameroon for the last 3 years, I was witness to the kidnappings of French citizens there, starting early last year, and then that has expanded. We have just had a third kidnapping earlier this year.

The kidnappings are part of this larger strategy of terror. And consistent with what the Lord's Resistance Army has done in Uganda, if I may venture it, I think they are actually copying the LRA's tactics, in some respects, which is why it is useful to have people from our military who are familiar with the LRA's tactics, in an attempt to apply that in Nigeria.

Senator FLAKE. Thank you.

My time is up.

Senator COONS. Thank you.

Senator Shaheen.

Senator SHAHEEN. Thank you, Mr. Chairman. And thank you, to you and Ranking Member Flake, for holding the hearing today.

As I think we would all agree, this kidnapping of these young girls in Nigeria is horrible, it is outrageous. We all are in sympathy with their families and the community that they came from. And it is been interesting to me to see the outcry around the world as the result of these kidnappings. And I think it, sadly, reminds us that there are too many girls and women around the world who are threatened, who are—for young girls who are just trying to get an education and better themselves, they are victims of violence. Too many children are given as child brides. Too many women are kidnapped and sold into slavery or sex trafficking. And we have got to do a better job, not only in the United States, but in the world, in combating these crimes.

And I know, this week, the International Violence Against Women Act was filed again. I am certainly hopeful that the full committee will take up this legislation and pass it, because we can either allow women to continue to be victims of violence and ignorance and repression or we can act on behalf of our wives, our daughters, our granddaughters and make a change in the world that will benefit everyone.

I wonder—and I am not sure who to direct this question to— I understand that there have been a number of offers of assistance to Nigeria—from France, from Britain; I understand that Israel and China have also offered to help. Can someone describe the extent to which those offers are being taken up and how the coordination is happening?

Ambassador JACKSON. Senator, I would be happy to take that question. In fact, we have a fusion cell, as we call it, in Abuja, the Nigerian capital, where the British, the French, the Americans, and the Nigerians are working together to develop the information that we have been able to gather through our various activities. We are also in touch with the Israelis and the Chinese, to a much lesser extent, but we are talking with them, to find out what is being provided. And I spoke with our team leader, just before coming to this hearing. He is very satisfied with the cooperation, and he is looking forward to expanding it this weekend, when the regional leaders meet in Paris.

Senator SHAHEEN. And are there any Muslim countries that have offered assistance?

Ambassador JACKSON. A number of Muslim countries have spoken out, and certainly Niger, which is predominantly Muslim, has offered its assistance to its neighbor, Nigeria, as has Chad.

Senator SHAHEEN. And when you say there are a number that have spoken out, have spoken out to condemn what has happened?

Ambassador JACKSON. Absolutely. And the message that all the Muslim leaders who have spoken out—whether religious leaders or political leaders, have passed is that this is not about Islam. And I think that is a very important point. Boko Haram's philosophy is not an Islamic philosophy.

Senator SHAHEEN. I agree, and I am glad that you made that point. Clearly, we need to make sure that Islam is not confused with some of these horrible terrorist acts that have been and continue to be perpetrated by terrorist groups.

Mr. Gast, can I ask you to elaborate a little bit on the question that Senator Coons posed about what we are doing to help address women and girls in Nigeria, where two-thirds of women in northern Nigeria receive no education, only 1 out of 20 women has a high school education, and where half of Nigerian women are reportedly married at age 15? Can you talk to what more we can do to address the circumstances there and cooperate with those organizations in Nigeria who share the values of trying to support getting an education for women?

Mr. GAST. Senator, I'd be pleased to take your question.

If one were to look at the development indicators between the north and south, it is almost looking at two different countries. And that is one of the reasons why we are targeting a lot of our assistance in health. In fact, 60 percent of that which is not related to the HIV/AIDS epidemic is targeted toward the north—the northwest as well as the northeast—and for education, as well, because we know that education access for AIDS are very low, and, in fact, in comparison with the rest of the continent, also near the bottom. And part of the problem is that educators themselves do not meet standards—less than 50 percent of the teachers in the north do not meet the federal standards.

So, we are helping the ministry with teachers' training, we are also helping with access to education.

The problem is—there are many problems, impediments along the way. One is security. And we do not want to do harm, we do not want to—in a very insecure environment, where we know Boko Haram is operating and where they are targeting girls, we do not want to encourage girls to go to schools. So, we are looking at alternative ways—at-home education, radio education, things of that sort.

We are also very focused, and we are supporting the government's program of saving 1 million lives, which is targeted toward maternal mortality and child mortality. And again——

Senator SHAHEEN. That is great.

Mr. GAST [continuing]. Both of those programs are in the north.

Senator SHAHEEN. And I guess—this is probably for Mr. Jackson—do you expect, or do we expect, either State or DOD to request additional funding to help with the situation in Nigeria?

Ambassador JACKSON. Senator, that is an excellent question. I think we will have to see how the operation evolves and how quickly we are able to develop good intelligence, based on our overflights. And we will get back to you.

Senator SHAHEEN. Thank you very much.

Thank you, Mr. Chairman.

Senator COONS. Thank you, Senator Shaheen.

Before I turn to Senator Rubio, I just want to remind all of us, we have a scheduled 11:15 vote. We have a second witness waiting to participate, live from Nigeria. And we will do what questions we can of her after hearing her opening statement.

Senator Rubio.

Senator RUBIO. Thank you, Mr. Chairman.

Thank you all for being here today and for your attention to this horrifying crime that has been committed.

Ambassador Jackson, from your testimony, from much of the media reporting on this, the perception is being created—and I wanted to ask you—is the prime motivator here of this instance, in your opinion—is the prime motivator the desire to deny young women access to education and empowerment?

Ambassador JACKSON. Senator, I actually think the prime motivator is to raise more funds for Boko Haram through a ransom. However, the fact that Boko Haram opposes Western education is certainly a reason why these girls were targeted.

Senator RUBIO. Well, can I suggest that I think there is another motivation that is not getting nearly enough attention? And that is that this is clearly motivated by an anti-Christian attitude of this group.

And I want to read you the comments from the leader of Boko Haram. I am sure you are aware of it, because the whole world has seen it. It is a grotesque statement. But, it is—basically, it concludes by saying, "To the people of the world, everybody should know his status. It is either you are with Mujahideen or you are with the Christians. We know what is happening in this world. It is a jihad war against Christians and Christianity. It is a war against Western education, democracy, and constitution. We have not started. Next time, we are going inside Abuja. We are going to a refinery and town of Christians. Do you know me? I have no problem with Jonathan. This is what I know in Quran, this is a war against Christians and democracy and their constitution. Allah says we should finish them when we get them."

I do not think there is any doubt about what is motivating them, or one of their leading motivators here is—this is not simply—and

I am—there is no doubt that this is a part of it, but this is not just about girls going to school, and it is not just about raising money. There is a strong anti-Christian element of this organization and of this activity. Am I right in saying that?

Ambassador JACKSON. Senator, there is a strong anti-Christian element, but I would offer that more of the thousands of people who have died as a result of Boko Haram's activities are Muslim than Christian.

Senator RUBIO. Well, again, I mean, I think when you commit these horrifying atrocities, you are going to target numerous people. But, from the very statement that he said, we should not ignore the fact that there is a religious-persecution aspect of this that is very significant and deserves attention, especially in light of what we are seeing, not just in this part of the world, but multiple areas of the world, where we are seeing horrifying instances of religious persecution against Christians, which, in my opinion, has been underreported.

So, would you agree that this is one such instance in which anti-Christian motivations are a strong component of what drives this organization to target—for example, my understanding is, according to one pastor, a Nigerian evangelist, most of the 200-plus schoolgirls kidnapped are Christians. Is that—so, clearly, anti-Christianity is a strong motivator in this effort.

Ambassador JACKSON. Senator, I respectfully suggest that, while anti-Christian sentiment is a strong motivator, the fact of the matter is that Boko Haram is trying to portray its philosophy as being a Muslim philosophy. And that is just not accurate. What both——

Senator RUBIO. I have not said it is a Muslim philosophy, but obviously it is a radical philosophy dressed up in a perversion of the tenets of a faith they claim to be adherents to.

I am not claiming that this is somehow driven by legitimate teachings of Islam. What I am arguing is that there is a strong anti-Christian element to this, and that it is part of a broader anti-Christian persecution that we are seeing repeatedly throughout the world. Would you disagree with that statement?

Ambassador JACKSON. I do not disagree, but I continue to want to emphasize that Boko Haram terrorizes all people.

Senator RUBIO. Okay. And I do not think that is in dispute. I guess my question is, just from the very statement that I have read here to you today, clearly he has featured Christianity as a key component that motivates who they are targeting and why they are targeting them.

Ambassador JACKSON. They are. But, if I may take the example of the schoolgirls, about 85 percent of the girls who were kidnapped were Christian, the other 15 percent were Muslim, but they are all hostages.

Senator RUBIO. Well, I just do not—okay, I do not—I think that we would stipulate that there are non-Christians that are being impacted by this, and it is horrifying just as well. A crime against Muslims is no less worse or less bad than a crime against Christians.

What I am trying to put aside—what I am trying to put forward here is that we cannot continue to ignore that persecution of Christians is a leading motivator, not just of what is happening in Boko

Haram, but in other parts of the world, as well, but, in this specific instance, they are clearly motivated by anti-Christian attitudes and anti-Christian beliefs. And I do not think that is even debatable, given their very own statement.

Here is my other question. In your opinion, in hindsight—and I know that hindsight's 20/20—was it a mistake not to designate this organization as a terrorist organization earlier?

Ambassador JACKSON. Senator, as I explained, I think we had a healthy debate. We are respectful of the Nigerian attitude toward Boko Haram and the fact that they feared that designating the organization would bring it more publicity. In retrospect, we might have done it earlier. I think the important thing is that we have done it and that we have offered a reward for the leadership of Boko Haram's location.

Senator RUBIO. I would just—for future reference, do you think there is a lesson here that, when we make decisions about designating groups as terrorists, they should not simply be—either you are a terrorist group or you are not, and that perhaps, in the future, we should not so heavily rely upon some government's input with regards to whether an organization that happens to be operating within their territory should be designated, or not? Is there any lessons there for the future?

Ambassador JACKSON. I think, Senator, that there is definitely a lesson here, and I think that we will be quicker to act to make designations based on our own assessments earlier on, based on this——

Senator RUBIO. Okay. And my last question has to do with a broader theme with regards to the risk of global jihadists and terrorism at large. There was a narrative not long ago—and I do not want to get into the politics of it—but, there was a narrative not long ago that al-Qaeda was on the run, that it was dissipating, but, in fact, what—a new risk has emerged, and this—want to rely, here, on the testimony of Director Clapper before the Senate Committee on Intelligence, of which I sit, where he said, ''The decentralization of al-Qaeda movement has led to the emergence of new power centers and an increase in threats by networks of like-minded extremists with allegiances to multiple groups,'' of which it is clear that AQIM, which is the—there appears to be some links or ties, at least with some elements of Boko Haram and Al Qaeda in the Islamic Maghreb.

So, my question is, What do we know, at this point, about that? Do we have any indications, at this stage, that you could reveal in a setting of this type, that, in fact, this is a group whose aspirations potentially involve attacks outside of Nigerian territory against Western interests either elsewhere in Africa or potentially in Europe and the Western world? What do we know about that at this stage?

Ambassador JACKSON. We have definitely determined that there are links between al-Qaeda and the Islamic Maghreb and Boko Haram. They have probably provided at least training, perhaps financial support. But, more importantly, to the second part of your question, Boko Haram has become a regional threat. It has kidnapped a French family in Cameroon, it has most recently kidnapped a Canadian priest—a Canadian nun and two Italian priests, and it kidnapped a French priest, several months ago, who was liberated. This is an organization that is becoming an international threat and needs to be dealt with through international cooperation.

Senator RUBIO. I just have a 15-second followup, Mr. Chairman.

Is it fair to begin to hold this—is it fair to hold this group up as yet another example of what Secretary Clapper was—Dr. Clapper was talking about, when he said that the decentralization of al-Qaeda and the emergence of these different groups in different regions poses the new face of the al-Qaeda threat in the 21st century? This group is just one more example of those types of groups that are popping up in different parts of the world that pose a different challenge in nature from the al-Qaeda we confronted during the 9/11 period.

Ambassador JACKSON. Senator, yes.

Senator RUBIO. Thank you.

Senator COONS. Thank you, Senator Rubio.

Chairman Menendez has returned. Do you have a question for this panel?

The CHAIRMAN. I do, Mr. Chairman, thank you very much. I was in a Banking markup, but appreciate the opportunity.

Let me ask you, Mr. Secretary. It is my understanding that Nigeria has not been cooperative with us in our efforts to designate Boko Haram as a terrorist group at the United Nations. Is that the case?

Ambassador JACKSON. Until very recently, they were very reluctant to designate them at the United Nations. However, this week their Permanent Representative did consult with the Security Council about designation, and I expect that will happen imminently.

The CHAIRMAN. Okay. So, we finally got them to see the light now. It is a shame that it took the abduction of 300 girls to get them to understand that they should have joined us at the United Nations.

But, you said "consulted." Does that mean that we are headed toward a designation? They are going to support us in our designation at the United Nations?

Ambassador JACKSON. Yes, Senator, we have been informed that they will work with us and other members of the Security Council to designate Boko Haram——

The CHAIRMAN. Good.

Ambassador JACKSON [continuing]. By the United Nations.

The CHAIRMAN. Well, that is a good development.

Now, we all want—even though the delay, I fear, may cause challenges to getting each and every one of these girls back, but that is our goal, and that is why I sent a letter to President Jonathan, calling on him to demonstrate leadership. But, what is your level of confidence that the Nigerian Government, after an indefensible delay, now has the political will and the military capacity to ensure a swift and effective response that utilizes international support to the fullest, and is in line with human rights standards?

Ambassador JACKSON. Senator, if I may, I will answer the political-will department and defer to my colleague for the Defense piece.

The CHAIRMAN. That is fine.

Ambassador JACKSON. We do believe that the political will now exists. President Jonathan is seized with the issue. In fact, I just learned, this morning, that he is on his way to Chibok to visit the school and meet with the families of the kidnapped girls.

Ms. FRIEND. Mr. Senator, if I may. After the social media campaign was underway in earnest, we found, in our engagements with the Nigerian military in particular, an unprecedented level of access and frankness with them. So, our impression from the Department of Defense is that they are quite certainly, for the first time in recent memory, taking this threat very seriously and engaging with us very seriously.

The CHAIRMAN. Well, what is their capacity? Because I see that we are spending a significant amount of money engaging them, in terms of creating capacity. I also see what happened at the school, and the notice they had and the lack of response. So, the question is, what is their capacity? Even if I accept that President Jonathan is now, because of international outrage, willing to do something, if we were to share, at some point, intelligence, assuming we had it and came upon it and could have actionable intelligence, what is their capacity to execute such an effort?

Ms. FRIEND. Senator, it is hard for me to answer that question right now, because we do not know what kind of situation we are facing, we cannot isolate particular courses of military action that might be appropriate for a rescue of the girls, because we do not know where they are.

There are two answers to your question. One is their capacity overall to handle the threat from Boko Haram, to take defensive measures, as you alluded to, at the school. There was also a recent prison-break equivalent at the Giwa barracks, I believe in March, that was virtually undefended by the Nigerian military. Again, as I spoke of earlier, the Nigerian military in the north has significant capacity challenges.

Our aim right now is to support them as much as possible, to get them training and assistance, where possible, and again——

The CHAIRMAN. Well, here is my problem, Ms.——

Ms. FRIEND [continuing]. We have an unprecedented level——

The CHAIRMAN. Here is my problem, Ms. Friend.

Ms. FRIEND [continuing]. Of cooperation.

The CHAIRMAN. We are going to support them as much as possible. But, if we found actionable intelligence that identified where a large part, or all, of the girls are, and we do not believe, or we do not know, if they have the capacity to act on it, what good will that be?

Ms. FRIEND. I cannot speculate on that, Senator. I do not want to give you speculative information. I do not——

The CHAIRMAN. Well——

Ms. FRIEND [continuing]. Know what kind of——

The CHAIRMAN [continuing]. That is a problem.

Ms. FRIEND [continuing]. Actionable information that might be.

The CHAIRMAN. I need you to go back to the Department and bring back to the committee a better answer than that.

Ms. FRIEND. I would be happy to, sir.

The CHAIRMAN. Because it is impossible to fathom that we might actually have actionable intelligence and that we would not have the wherewithal, either by the Nigerians themselves, or by other entities helping the Nigerians, to be able to conduct a rescue mission. And so, all of this would be worthless unless we know the Nigerians are capable of executing, or, in the absence of their ability to execute, that we have some other way to be able to effectuate an effective rescue.

So, I would like for you to go back to the Department, at whatever level is necessary, to give the committee a better answer than that, because, otherwise, some of us will question all of our efforts if they cannot be executed upon.

Ms. FRIEND. Sir, as we gather more information with the Nigerians, we would be happy to come back and talk to you about that.

The CHAIRMAN. Well, I would like, yes, from the Nigerians, but I want to know our own assessment. I want to have the Department of Defense's assessment as to what would be the capacity of the Nigerian military and/or security to effectuate a rescue mission, assuming that that opportunity unveils itself. We are not going to wait until finding out that we have actionable intelligence and then find out we do not have the capacity to do this.

Ms. FRIEND. I would be happy to come back to you with that information, sir.

The CHAIRMAN. Wow.

Thank you, Mr. Chairman.

Senator COONS. Chairman Menendez, any further questions?

We are trying to work out the logistics of a vote that is about to be called, and a second-panel witness. Senator Cardin has questions for this panel. At the forbearance of the witnesses, I am going to invite Senator Cardin to question this panel. Senator Flake and I are going to go to the floor, cast our votes, and come promptly back, and Senator Cardin will transition to the introduction of our witness if we are not back within 7 minutes, which I suspect we will be.

Senator CARDIN. And I do not expect to take 7 minutes, so I will keep it moving.

Senator COONS. We will move as quickly as we can.

Senator CARDIN [presiding]. Right. I understand the challenges. As I think the chairman has pointed out, the floor has a series of votes starting at 11:15, so I will do my best to keep things moving along.

This is a matter of urgency globally, as I think has been expressed here. These Nigerian girls were not in the wrong place at the wrong time, they were in the right place at the right time. And what happened there is just beyond description.

So, this is not a U.S. interest, this is a global humanitarian interest. The United States has certain unique capabilities, and the international community has certain capabilities. We are not yet clear as to the capacity of the Nigerian Government to act. We do believe that the international focus on this issue has given greater strength to the Nigerian Government to take the appropriate steps to ensure the safe return of the girls.

So, I was listening to the comments of my colleagues, and I know it is frustrating when we know how long these girls have been held captive. So, I guess my only observation, not so much as a question, is that this is not about what we read in the paper, this is about getting the girls back safely. This is not about the United States or the United States being visible or invisible. It is about getting the girls home safely. And we want to do everything we possibly can in that regard.

There is also the issue, generally in Nigeria, of how they handle opposition, how they handle the stability in their own country, which is of concern to the United States. And what I think most of us are concerned about is that we do not want the safety of these girls confused with the outrageous terrorist acts and we do not want to give these actors any legitimacy whatsoever. And I think that is a point that, again, it is not just U.S. interests, but it is a matter of global humanitarian interest. So, this is that balance that we are seeking. How can we be constructive and how can we be forceful in helping bring back these girls safely?

And I thank you all for your testimonies today. And we know these are difficult, anxious moments. But, we want to be as constructive as we possibly can. We want to be very clear about the outrageous conduct of terrorists that go beyond the pale of anything any of us can imagine and that we recognize that this is a global matter that the Nigerians must handle, but they should seek help from the international community, and we are ready to assist.

Thank you all very much.

I would now invite up Ms. Lantana Abdullahi. I assume I mispronounced that.

STATEMENT OF LANTANA ABDULLAHI, PROJECT MANAGER, SEARCH FOR COMMON GROUND, JOS, NIGERIA

Ms. ABDULLAHI [via videocast from Nigeria]. Hello. Members of the Senate. Ladies and gentlemen, good morning. Hello?

Senator CARDIN. We hear you fine. Can you hear us?

Ms. ABDULLAHI. Oh, good. Members of the Senate—Ladies and gentlemen, good morning. Chairman Coons, Ranking Member Flake, members of the committee, thank you for convening this important and timely meeting and for giving me the opportunity to speak today.

I thank other witnesses today—Honorable Mr. Jackson, Honorable Mr. Gast, and Ms. Friend—for their all testimonies. I thank all of you for your leadership, commitment, and efforts to help Nigerians respond to the growing crisis in our country.

My name is Lantana Abdullahi, and I work on country transformation and violence prevention with Search for Common Ground in Nigeria. The testimony that follows reflects my own views and informed by my experiences first as a mother with five children, as a Nigerian, and as a peace-builder.

I will begin by briefly speaking how on the events that have brought us here today, the causes of the current crisis, and offer some practical recommendations.

You will all recall that today marks the 30th day that is over 200 Christian and Muslim girls were abducted from a school in Chibok, north Nigeria. Of course this means a whole generation is apparently at risk. This is only one of many attacks which Boko Haram has claimed responsibility.

The group was created in 2002 with the sole purpose of imposing a version of Islamic law throughout Nigeria. So far, the attacks have claimed more than 2,000 people, to date, and displaced tens of thousands of people, and more than 10 million people are currently at risk if you combine the population of Adamawa, Yobe, and Borno states.

And, in addition to one of the comments made about the goal of Boko Haram, about their anti-Christianity stance, I want to say that, of course, it is a ploy to pit Christians and Muslims against each other, and, of course, also seek, sympathy among some Muslims.

This abduction just serves as a reminder, a sad reminder, of the longstanding challenges at play in Nigeria that may also produce a negative impact throughout the greater region. Currently, the lack of information on the current level of response from the government and armed forces is a great source of worry for many Nigerians. Nigerians are also very much frustrated by the history and current level of corruption in the government, associated, of course, with bad governance and impunity.

Boko Haram argues that corruption is the result of democracy, a Western import that has failed. This description resonates well with marginalized groups if you look at their recruitment efforts and rife.

Northern Nigeria, as we all know, has been historically disadvantaged, in comparison to the south—to the more developed south. Boko Haram took advantage of this to make inroads with local population by offering food, shelter, and free Quranic education. We must also acknowledge the porous nature of our borders near Borno, Yobe, and Adamawa states, where violence has originated and allowed Boko Haram to traffic victims as well as escape prosecution by seeking refuge abroad.

We have all been deeply touched by the attention—of the girls' kidnapping—that has been received, but I think there is still a need for more to be done to end this crisis. Affected citizens have on-the-ground response. While securing the girls' release will be a short-term gain, ensuring lasting peace in the region requires the militancy issue to be addressed from multiple angles with engagement of all stakeholders to prevent future atrocities.

Despite the recent escalation of Boko Haram violent actions, there are a few reasons to be hopeful. First, we have witnessed a decrease in reprisal attacks, especially coming from regions like the north central Nigeria, and in particular, plateau state, Jos, where I come from.

During earlier periods of the insurgency, victims appealed to their own communities to gain retribution. More recently, we have seen more and more Christians and Muslims working together, as seen by the #BringBackOurGirls movement, and driven, as was seen, of course, by Nigerians.

In the past, there has been poor international coordination. However, the global attention generated by the abduction of these girls and the World Economic Forum for Africa, hosted in Nigeria, have created an opportunity for the United States and other foreign technical assistance.

With this in mind, I will want to make the following recommendations. There is an urgent need for humanitarian assistance and support to prevent further marginalization of the populations who are at risk of being recruited into militancy. There is also urgent need for trauma counseling and psychosocial support to victims of violence in northeast Nigeria.

Other recommendations support an original approach. Like all other witnesses have said, there is a need to have a regional collaboration between Nigeria and its neighbors, particularly Niger Republic, Cameroon, and Chad. Securing the borders will limit terrorist activities and prevent the spread of militancy. We need also to support a robust community-focused approach to improving human security. How do we ensure communities are also engaged in this? We also need to prevent and monitor human rights abuses by security forces. More importantly, we know that the level of presence of military and armed forces in most conflict locations have also increased the level of violations of human rights of citizens. We need to consolidate the gains in peace-building effort throughout Nigeria.

Inasmuch as we want to concentrate on the current crisis in the northeast region particularly on the Boko Haram terrorist activities, we should not also forget the issues in the Niger Delta, the middle—and, of course, the upcoming general elections.

I would like to close with a personal story. Three years ago, I was at a wedding in Maiduguri, Boko Haram's place of birth. As soon as I arrived, I heard multiple explosions, serving as a painful reminder of the violence affecting the residents. Their ability to move freely was heavily restricted. Even during joyous celebrations, they were constantly made aware of the lack of security. Yet, it also warmed my heart to see how resilient my family were, as well as their friends and neighbors. Despite the terror, women still went to the market, and children courageously still attended school. My visit to Maiduguri strengthened my commitment as a peace-builder to ensure that all Nigerians, both Christians and Muslims, can work together and live free of fear.

I tell you this story to remind you that my experience is not unique. Millions of other people throughout northeastern Nigeria and, indeed, Nigeria are affected by this violence. I hope my testimony today represents them all.

I also want to thank the U.S. Senate for this opportunity to speak and for showing interest to support us to overcome these challenges. In particular, I also wish to appreciate and thank the American people for joining the global movement to #BringBackOurGirls and end terrorism. We must continue in this spirit until the war is won.

Thank you, and I await your questions.

[The prepared statement of Ms. Abdullahi follows:]

PREPARED STATEMENT OF LANTANA ADBULLAHI

Members of the Senate, ladies, and gentlemen, good morning. Chairman Coons, Ranking Member Flake, members of the committee, I would like to begin by thanking you for convening this important and timely meeting, and for giving me the opportunity to speak today on this crisis. I also thank the Honorable Mr. Jackson, Hon. Ms. Gast, and Ms. Friend for their testimonies today. I thank all of you for your leadership, commitment, and efforts to help Nigerians respond to the growing crisis in our country.

My name is Lantana Abdullahi and I work on conflict transformation and violence prevention with Search for Common Ground in Nigeria. Since 2004, we have been developing innovative media and community projects that encourage mutual understanding across ethnic, religious, and gender lines. I recently led a project to empower Muslim and Christian girls from northern Nigeria and promote them as peacebuilders, and currently work with communities, women, youth, and civil soci- ety groups to prevent violence and promote peace. The testimony that follows reflects my own views, which are informed by my experiences as a mother, a Nige- rian, as well as a peace-builder.

I will begin by speaking briefly on the events that have brought us together today, some of the causes of the current crisis, and conclude with some practical actions that can be taken in order to respond to the immediate crisis and bring about long-term solutions.

THE CURRENT STATE OF AFFAIRS

On April 14, 2014, the Islamist militant group Boko Haram abducted more than 200 girls from a school in Chibok, a town in northeastern Nigeria. While the identity of the girls is still being confirmed, the abductees included both Muslim and Christian girls. This abduction was just one of the latest attacks for which the militant group Boko Haram has claimed responsibility. The group began its insurgency in 2009, with the aim of imposing its own version of Islamic law throughout Nigeria. In the past 5 years, the group has targeted the United Nations headquarters in Abuja, churches, the police, markets, and schools throughout northeastern Nigeria, and has regularly engaged in bloody combat with the Nigerian military and police forces. These attacks have led to over 3,000 deaths—(World Report 2013: Nigeria)— a state of emergency declaration in May 2013 in three northeastern states, and the displacement of tens of thousands of my fellow citizens. In all, Boko Haram's actions have affected more than 10 million people. It risks becoming a regional crisis, and placing serious strains on Nigeria's relations with neighboring Niger, Cameroon, and Chad.

UNDERLYING CHALLENGES

The abduction of the Chibok school girls last month is a sad escalation of the terror the Nigerian people have witnessed since 2009. This crisis comes as a result of four long-running challenges that not only affect the northeastern parts of the country, but have the possibility to produce widespread impact across all of Nigeria and in the neighboring countries.

The first challenge is that of corruption and lack of confidence in government in Nigeria. Many Nigerians are frustrated, and feel that there is a high degree of corruption in the country. Boko Haram argues that corruption is the result of democracy and Western influences. According to this argument, democracy is a Western import that has not succeeded in Nigeria. Past elections have resulted in violence, and militants argue that this contradicts the principles of Islamic sharia law—given by God. This has a certain resonance with frustrated, poor, and desperate people who perceive a growing gap between rich and poor, and suspect that politicians are using their public offices to secure private wealth.

The second challenge is chronic poverty. This is of particular concern in northern Nigeria, which is historically disadvantaged with regards to the more developed south. The effects of poverty on the population are pervasive: without a strong economy or income-generating activities, many parents send their children to the only schools available. An exclusively Koranic school education without other practical training offers limited opportunities for students when they graduate—as it leaves out subjects such as mathematics, science, and the liberal arts—leaving them unprepared and unable to find adequate employment. Thus these youngsters are more susceptible to recruitment into violent groups. Additionally, Boko Haram first made in-roads with the local population by offering food and shelter, thereby taking advantage of people's vulnerability as a result of poverty.

The third challenge stems from the geographical location of the Boko Haram insurgency. Borno, Yobe, and Adamawa states—where this violence has originated— are located along Nigeria's border with Niger, Chad, and Cameroon. Weak borders and governance in the remote region allow for the trafficking of individuals and arms across countries. Boko Haram can not only facilitate the trafficking of victims, but it can also escape persecution and seek refuge in neighboring countries when the situation becomes too precarious for them in Nigeria.

Finally, these challenges go hand in hand with the lack of a strong civil society and media presence. In recent years, many different local and international organizations have been moving to the region but have yet to deliver a strong impact. Media programs and outlets continue to have limited reach compared to the rest of the country, and citizens have few opportunities to make their voices heard on national issues. Consequently, the local population does not trust available news sources, leaving no suitable outlets for popular expression.

Key Opportunities and Recommendations

I have been deeply touched by the attention the tragedy of the Chibok Girls' kidnapping has garnered both in Nigeria and in the world. Their kidnapping comes after a long wave of killings, kidnappings, and abuses, and underscores the need for new approaches to the crisis. Thus far, citizens living in the most-affected areas have seen little on-the-ground response to the crisis apart from the current offensive undertaken by security forces. Yet despite these operations, the insurgency persists, and human rights groups have presented grave reports of extremely serious abuses committed by the security actors. While securing the girls' release will be a short-term gain, ensuring lasting peace in the region requires the militancy issue be addressed from multiple angles. It also requires the engagement of all stake-holders—communities, civil society, government, and its international partners—to ensure context-specific and sustainable solutions to improve human security, peacebuilding, and the prevention of future atrocities.

While the violent actions perpetrated by Boko Haram have increased in scale, quantity, frequency, there are a few reasons to be hopeful.

First, we have witnessed a decrease in reprisal violence within affected communities. During earlier periods of the insurgency, victims of violence appealed to their own communities, often divided along religious and ethnic lines, in order to attain justice or retribution. Recently we have seen more and more Christians and Muslims working together, supporting one another, and recognizing the need to unite to prevent violence. With the #Bringbackourgirls campaign, we have also seen a more concerted effort by Nigerians across the country to recognize the tragic consequences of the conflict in the northeast.

Secondly, in the past, there has been poor coordination with the international community, as well as with neighboring countries. However, the global attention generated by the abductions of the girls and the campaign by CSOs, as well as the World Economic Forum for Africa hosted in Nigeria, have created an opportunity for foreign technical assistance from the U.S., UK, and France.

These two changes present an opportunity for the U.S. Government to support Nigerians as they try to respond to this crisis.

The challenges and opportunities call for a running engagement and specific actions to face longstanding problems. With this in mind, I make the recommendation for practical courses of action.

The first set is focused on addressing the human consequences of the current crisis in three key ways:

a. *There is an immediate need for trauma healing and psychosocial support to victims of violence in northeast Nigeria.* The psychological legacies of violence will create long-term scars, both for these girls, as well as the thousands of their fellow citizens who have lost loved ones, experienced abuses, lost their homes, and otherwise suffered as a result of the violence.

b. *There is an urgent need for humanitarian support.* Tens of thousands of people have fled in fear, becoming refugees in neighboring countries and fleeing to other parts of Nigeria. In some places the influx of refugees has overtaxed local water and food supplies, overcrowded schools and clinics, and competes with locals for economic opportunities. There is a need to ensure the protection of women and children fleeing the violence, to ensure they are not exposed to sexual exploitation. There is a need to work with the displaced people to ensure that in their desperation, they do not themselves become recruited into militancy and violence.

c. *Finally, there is need to begin planning for early recovery.* The Nigerian Government and its international partners should begin working with local communities to begin planning for how to rebuild from the devastation, including repairing infrastructure and homes that have been destroyed, creating economic livelihoods opportunities, and implementing emergency programs, such as catchup education programs for those whose schooling has been disrupted by war.

Even while addressing its consequences, the international community can also undertake specific steps to help bring the crisis to an end in four ways:

a. *Support a regional approach to prevent the Boko Haram militancy from becoming a broader crisis.* There needs to be regional collaboration to work with border communities and governments to improve security along the borders between Nigeria, Niger, Cameroon, and Chad. The porous borders between these countries have facilitated human trafficking, arms and drug trade, and the movement of mercenaries. Securing the borders will limit terrorist activities and prevent the spread of militancy. The regional collaboration should not be limited to the formal security forces, but can involve local leaders, civil society, media, and governments in all four countries to recognize a shared interest in more secure and productive communities, with a particular focus on youth. Actions can include strategic livelihoods programming, community empowerment, and supporting pluralistic platforms for dialogue on diversity and tolerance through the media sector.

b. *Allocate adequate funding to support a robust community-focused approach to improving human security in northeastern Nigeria.* The U.S. strategy to support northeastern Nigeria should focus on empowering women, youth, local leaders and religious groups within the conflict-affected areas of the northeast. Building cohesive, empowered, and resilient local communities will help reduce the risk of recruitment, create alternative ways for local residents to raise their concerns to government officials, and help reduce the risk of recruitment of young people. Such an approach should also include civil society capacity-building and media engagement to document security conditions and monitor allegations of human rights abuses.

c. *Work with civil society, religious and local leaders, Nigerian authorities, the security forces and the National Human Rights Commission to prevent and monitor human rights abuses.* This includes providing support platform building to strengthen relationships between civil society groups and the NHRC to prevent abuses in the north. Operations have been marked by reports of grave human rights abuses, and ensuring that there is a transparent process for addressing these grievances, agreed upon by all stakeholders, will prevent the allegations of abuses from becoming new grievances.

d. *Consolidate the gains in peace-building throughout Nigeria.* Alongside the crisis in the northeast, Nigeria is facing a series of other violent conflicts in the Niger Delta, as well as in the Middle Belt. Additionally, the nation will be looking forward to elections next year. Even as we focus on resolving the crisis in the northeast, it is critical that sufficient funds should be allocated to continue to support the consolidation of peace in the Niger Delta, interfaith peace efforts in the Middle Belt, and support the electoral process.

CONCLUSION

I would like to close with a personal story. Three years ago, I was in Maiduguri. As soon as I arrived, I was shocked to hear explosions all around us, serving as a painful reminder of the violence that my relatives, friends, and fellow citizens are subjected to on a regular basis. Witnessing the routine violation of my relatives' rights and liberty particularly saddened me. Their ability to move freely was heavily restricted—even during joyous celebrations they were constantly made aware of their lack of freedom. Yet it also warmed my heart of see how resilient my family was, as well as their friends, neighbors, and communities. Despite the terror, women still went to the market. Children courageously still attended school. My fellow Nigerians were going about their lives in spite of the violence that surrounded them.

My visit to Maiduguri strengthened my commitment to work as a peace-builder in Nigeria, to ensure that all Nigerians, both Christians and Muslims, can work together and live free of fear. I am reminded today that my experience is not unique and millions of people throughout northeastern Nigeria are affected by violence and gross violations of their individual rights and freedoms.

Thank you once again for giving this opportunity and for your interest in supporting us to overcome the challenges facing our country.

Senator COONS [presiding]. Thank you very much for your testimony, Lantana Abdullahi. We are grateful for you joining us today.

You have experienced so much as someone from the north and as an advocate for peace-building. How has Boko Haram impacted your life, the community around you in the north? And what message would you like to send to the perpetrators of these vicious attacks?

Ms. ABDULLAHI. I think I want to talk, first, as a Muslim. I want to say the activities of Boko Haram has actually affected almost all Muslims, you know, in Nigeria, because we have been left to actually start, you know, talking about defending our faith and, you know, educating and sensitizing people that Boko Haram do not actually represent Islam and do not represent the interests of Muslims in Nigeria.

And, of course, coming from where we are, we are dealing with other conflicts in other locations, like the north-central region, where we are dealing more with issues of ethnic and religious conflicts. You know, Boko Haram has also taken advantage of that to also try to, you know, perpetrate some of the terrorist activities, you know, in some of these locations, and it has taken, you know, a lot of, you know, our efforts to make sure we localize the context and not allow Boko Haram to actually hijack the process and the work we are doing in Nigeria.

Senator COONS. Thank you.

As you know, many Americans have taken to the Internet to express their outrage with Boko Haram and their support for safely returning—for bringing back the girls. And today's hearing is an expression, in part, of American concern and solidarity and commitment to support the families and the girls. What message do you have for us, for the U.S. Government and the American people, as we consider what more we could do to support peace and security in Nigeria?

Ms. ABDULLAHI. I think, very importantly, we want to acknowledge the American people and government for coming to our rescue at this moment. We know of the military cooperation currently going on between America and Nigerian Government. Even though, of course, the support of the—from Nigerian Government for such support is coming late, but we still believe that the time is now to actually act.

And, in particular, we also need to look at other nonmilitary support from the American Government, particularly when we are looking at other community-driven, peace-building strategies and approach to also consolidate on the post-abduction stage. We need to do that to rebuild the communities, but, more importantly, we need to acknowledge that the northeast region is the one of the most backward, you know, regions in Nigeria. There is, you know, a weak media presence, there is weak civil society presence, and this means that we need to actually push to empowered communities to speak their voice, not to allow some people or institutions to speak for them. So, that is why we are pushing to see how we can have community-level, you know, -driven radio stations, even though, at this moment, there is actually no license. The government is not issuing such license. But, we think that the time has come to have community radios to work with young girls and to work with also women and youth.

Senator COONS. Well, thank you for those comments.

If you could tell us what other initiatives, in addition to the radio conversation, that your organization, the organization for which you work, Search for Common Ground, has taken. And, as a peacebuilder, Lantana, what are the most important steps you have taken to encourage reconciliation and dialogue amongst the communities in the north? What are the most positive steps you have seen so far? And what recommendations do you have for us about how we can best support peace-building efforts in the north?

Ms. ABDULLAHI. As you know, Search for Common Ground is an organization that is very innovative. It meets peace-building efforts around the world. And that innovation and uniqueness is what we have brought to deal with conflicts in many parts of Nigeria. Currently, we are working basically more in the middle belt region, trying to bring, you know, ethnic groups together to look at their common grounds values, and to work on their differences. We are also, of course, supporting the federal government to work on the militancy problem and stability in the Niger delta region. We have been supporting communities to sit and, you know, dialogue over their differences using their own local initiatives. We have also been empowering them with skills and knowledge, particularly on conflict transformation, to be able to deal with those issues constructively.

Senator COONS. Thank you, Lantana.

I am going to yield to Senator Flake so that he also has an opportunity to ask questions before we must return for our next vote.

Thank you so much for your testimony today.

Senator Flake.

Senator FLAKE. Well, thank you. And I am sorry if I am asking questions that have already been answered.

But, with regard to the government's response to what is going on in the north, have there been any initiatives by the government that have been effective in diminishing the attractiveness of Boko Haram for recruiting or for their activities? Is the government winning this battle, or not, at this point?

Ms. ABDULLAHI. Of course, it is obvious that if young—you know, over 200 young girls can actually be abducted right, you know, in the presence of the Nigerian Government, and remain missing for 30 days, it means that we have lost it somewhere. It is obvious that there is still some lack of capacity to actually deal with the problem we are currently facing. It also seems that, since the advent of the Boko Haram in 2002, the government were not actually prepared to actually deal with the issue. And, of course, they have, for us, most Nigerians, there have been many analysts, many arguments, about, you know, the position of government on using just, you know, the military offensive to deal with the Boko Haram in suggest the—instead of, you know, trying to address some of the root causes, you know, that brought about the advent of Boko Haram in the first instance.

Of course, recently, we have had some announcements by the government about, you know, some grants to northeast region to try to provide some sustainable and livelihoods—you know, address some of the livelihood and concerns of the region, to address the widespread poverty and the low educational level and political, you know, marginalization of that region. But, of course, we have also not seen anything happening in regard to the money that was meant for that.

Senator FLAKE. One other question. I think we were struck, here, and the international community was struck, at how slow the Nigerian Government reacted to these kidnappings. Does that suggest that they simply are not ready and willing to address the issues, whether they are the root causes or more immediate concerns? And are they only acting because the international community is putting pressure on them now?

Ms. ABDULLAHI. Yes, I think that they were slow, of course, you know, responding to the crisis. And, of course, we also have to acknowledge the role played by Nigerians. They have been daily, you know, coming out to actually push and, you know, talk about the current, you know, crisis.

Of course, we also have to acknowledge that there have been many, you know, push by the international community to come in and support, but the government were very skeptical, they were very, you know, slow in accepting those offers. But, I think Nigerians have actually pushed for that, and we have seen it, you know, happening now, and we hope that, apart from just wanting to have the girls released, we also want, beyond, you know, the abduction, to address, you know, those root causes.

Senator FLAKE. All right. Thank you. I will turn it back to the chairman. Thank you for your participation. We really appreciate you doing this.

Ms. ABDULLAHI. Thank you so much.

Senator COONS. So, Ms. Abdullahi, if you have any closing comments you would like to make to us—we have to go back to the Senate floor in just a moment for another vote. I know it was a little disjointed, between Senator Cardin, Senator Flake, and myself. If there is any closing comments you have for us, suggestions about how we can most be helpful in supporting reconciliation and development in the north that will address some of the root causes of the Boko Haram insurgency or that can address some of the root causes of violence and of difficulties between communities, I would welcome that. And if you have any other suggestions for how we can best support the Nigerian schoolgirls who have been kidnapped and their families, we would welcome that, as well.

Thank you so much for your testimony. We look forward to a closing comment from you.

Ms. ABDULLAHI. Thank you so much for the opportunity to actually talk today. And, of course, like I said, we need a lot of support. There is currently weak presence of the civil society on ground to actually support the current crisis in the region, so we want the U.S. Senate to push to see how we can have more of the civil actions going on right now in the region by, you know, sorting out the humanitarian issues immediately, but also looking out to plan long-term interventions, working with youth groups, women groups, and young girls to promote civilian protection and also promote human rights respect by armed forces and also on a community-driven approach.

Senator COONS. Thank you so much. Thank you for your focus on peace-building, on respecting human rights, and on reconciliation. We are grateful——

Ms. ABDULLAHI. Thank you.

Senator COONS [continuing]. For the effort that you made to testify before us today.

I will leave the record open for an additional week, until the close of business, Thursday, May 22, for any members of this committee who were not able to attend but who have questions either for our first or second panel.

We greatly appreciate the testimony that was offered today by all four of our witnesses and the very hard work that many are doing here in the Capitol of the United States to provide support and assistance to the Nigerian schoolgirls and their families, to the people of Nigeria, and to all who are working for peace and reconciliation in Nigeria.

Thank you. And, with that, this hearing is adjourned.

[Whereupon, at 11:35 a.m., the hearing was adjourned.]

ADDITIONAL MATERIAL SUBMITTED FOR THE RECORD

RESPONSES OF AMBASSADOR ROBERT P. JACKSON TO QUESTIONS SUBMITTED BY SENATOR CHRISTOPHER A. COONS

Question. Human Rights Violations.—To what degree has Nigeria's poor track record with regard to human rights limited bilateral cooperation with the military and police? What steps has the Nigerian Government taken to address this issue. Specifically, how have Leahy restrictions on U.S. security assistance limited assistance offered to Nigeria's police and military in the past, and what are the current plans for providing military and police support moving forward?

Answer. The military's heavy-handed approach to combating Boko Haram and the resulting gross violations of human rights have prevented the United States from assisting some units. Nevertheless, despite these challenges, we continue to work with eligible units to help the Nigerian Government to locate and liberate the kidnapped school girls, and to combat Boko Haram. In 2013, we vetted and approved 1,108 individuals and units from the Nigerian security forces that were nominated to receive training, equipment, and other forms of assistance. There are currently 187 Nigerian military units and 173 Nigerian police units that have been Leahy vetted and approved, and are cleared to receive U.S. assistance and training, including soldiers from Nigeria's elite Special Boat Service (SBS) commando unit, the 101st and 143rd counterterrorism units.

We help the Nigerian Government professionalize its military and security services, improve its ability to participate in peacekeeping operations and conduct maritime security to improve its counterimprovised explosive device (IED) capacity, and carry-out responsible and effective counterterrorism (CT) operations. We also provide law enforcement assistance, including by training Nigerian law enforcement officials on CT investigations, border security, counter IED and post-blast investigations, tactical operations, and crisis management. All of this assistance is part of a coordinated effort to help strengthen Nigeria's ability to respond responsibly and effectively to their security challenges in a way that ensures civilians are protected, human rights are respected, and violators are held accountable in accordance with the Leahy law and our foreign policy objectives.

We have referenced the Leahy law in engaging with senior-level Nigerian officials, in our efforts to encourage the Nigerian Government to adopt a smarter approach to fighting Boko Haram and to professionalize their forces. These efforts have led to difficult but productive discussions on the damage that human rights violations can do to counterinsurgency and counterterrorism efforts, and the importance of accountability for those responsible. We have seen some signs of progress, like President Jonathan's February 24 order to include more human rights training for officers, but we expect more as we continue to engage Nigerians on these challenging issues while also providing assistance in critical areas in accordance with our laws and policies.

Under the Leahy laws, and consistent with U.S. policy to seek rights-respecting security partners, we do not provide assistance, including training, to security force units when we have credible information that they have committed gross violations of human rights, including extrajudicial killings, enforced disappearance, rape, and torture, unless the host government is taking effective steps to bring those responsible to justice. Even if the Leahy Law did not exist, we recognize that such abuses undermine the fight against Boko Haram by alienating the civilians that the Nigerian military and security services should be protecting, and whose allegiance the Nigerian Federal Government needs to defeat the terrorists.

The U.S. decision to provide assistance to any military, security, or law enforcement unit is driven both by overall policy considerations as well as the Leahy laws. We continue to urge the Nigerian Government to adopt a comprehensive counterterrorism strategy that includes action both to hold the perpetrators of human violations accountable and to curtail further human rights abuses by security forces. Such actions by the Nigerian Government will also allow us to deepen our partnership with the Nigerian Government in its fight against Boko Haram.

Question. Police.—You mentioned in your testimony that you are providing law enforcement basic forensics, hostage negotiations, leadership, and task force development. When did this assistance begin? It does not appear that International Narcotics Control and Law Enforcement (INCLE) funds were requested for Nigeria in FY13, FY14, or FY15. Given the important role played by the police in civilian protection, why hasn't U.S. police assistance been prioritized for Nigeria, and what police assistance is planned moving forward?

Answer. Since 2012, the Department has provided law enforcement and rule of law INCLE-funded assistance to Nigeria under the West Africa Cooperative Security Initiative (WACSI), a whole-of-government effort to increase global security by addressing transnational organized crime in West Africa. WACSI receives International Narcotics Control and Law Enforcement (INCLE) funds under the State Africa Regional account (funded in the West Africa Regional Security Initiative Program line), rather than a bilateral INCLE funding line for Nigeria.

In recent discussions with INL, high-level Nigerian Police Force officials expressed willingness to engage on institutional reform at their training academies. Future INL programming will focus on building the long-term institutional capacity of the police to perform their duties, while meeting international standards and human rights norms. As part of this effort, INL plans to initiate a Police Training Modernization project at Nigerian police academies in late 2014 and a regional project to facilitate community and police dialogues utilizing Trans-Sahara Counterterrorism Partnership (TSCTP) funding allocated for police reform in Nigeria.

RESPONSES OF AMBASSADOR ROBERT P. JACKSON TO QUESTIONS
SUBMITTED BY SENATOR BENJAMIN L. CARDIN

Question. While there is strong civil society and interreligious commitments to peace-building elsewhere in Nigeria, there has been little on-the-ground response to the crisis in northeastern Nigeria apart from the security forces.

A security-only approach has led to both an out-of-control insurgency and atrocious human rights abuses, and as we've seen time and again across the Middle East and North Africa, including in Mali, will not successfully counter violent extremism. And yet, since the global public outrage on the abduction of the school girls, the administration has focused disproportionately on security assistance to the Government of Nigeria.

- ◆ How are we supporting local civil society organizations, including local and international interreligious and peace-building organizations, to ensure a balanced, well-rounded approach to protect civilians from and prevent the further emboldening of Boko Haram?
- ◆ What are some of the major underlying grievances among civilian populations in northern Nigeria and what can the U.S. do to help address these challenges?
- ◆ How have issues related to resource-scarcity and climate-impacted communities throughout Nigeria and particularly in the north?

Answer. The administration continues to press the Nigerian Government to implement a comprehensive approach to combating violent extremism and insecurity in northeastern Nigeria that addresses the underlying causes of the conflict and grievances of northern populations while concomitantly emphasizing civilian protection, respect for human rights, the rule of law, and accountable security forces.

Operating in the poorest part of Nigeria, Boko Haram exploits the northern population's legitimate grievances to garner recruits and support. Heavily reliant on subsistence agriculture, the Northeast already faces issues of resource scarcity and climate change. However, the population's most serious grievances include lack of employment, infrastructure, sanitation, health care, education, and political marginalization. Corruption, patronage networks, and weak institutions have resulted in the systemic poor performance of the Federal, State, and local governments to meet basic citizen needs. These unfulfilled demands are exacerbated when resources allocated to address these issues are misappropriated, also impeding development and investment. Heavy-handed tactics by security forces against the civilian population has tended further compound the alienation from the government of people living in northeast Nigeria.

We are taking a number of steps to help alleviate these grievances:

- • We are working with the Nigerian Government to more effectively engage communities vulnerable to extremist violence and promote practices among its security forces that protect civilians, respect human rights, and do not further alienate already aggrieved communities.

- The U.S. Embassy supports local religious leaders who reach across sectarian lines and promote human rights, social justice, and conflict resolution. USAID has conducted conflict mitigation and management interventions to lessen sectarian and intercommunal tensions and to increase interfaith civic engagement and tolerance among flashpoint communities.
- USAID is helping to strengthen education management systems; improve the reading skills of 5.5 million northern Nigerian primary school students; improve the quality of education for teachers to teach reading, and increase access of orphans and vulnerable children, including itinerant Qur'anic youth (Almajiri), and girls, to basic education. These programs focus on the northern states of Bauchi and Sokoto.
- USAID is supporting economic growth and poverty alleviation by improving agricultural productivity and expanding jobs in the rural sector through the Feed the Future initiative.
- Through President Obama's "Power Africa" initiative, the United States will continue to partner with Nigeria to ensure that the Nigerian people have greater access to electricity.
- In the health sector in northern Nigeria, USAID supports increased access to quality family planning, immunization, and maternal health services. USAID also supports efforts to decrease the number of malaria-related deaths in pregnant women and children by increasing access to treatment, insecticide-treated bed nets, and retreatment kits. USAID provides HIV/AIDs prevention, care, and treatment services as well as services to orphans and vulnerable children.
- We are working with civil society to advance transparent and accountable governance. In 2013, the State Department launched a 2-year pilot program to build the capacity of civil society (including media) to increase citizens' access to government-held information.
- USAID works with state and local governments to improve budget preparation and fiscal oversight to ensure adequate service delivery. Working with a diverse group of civil society organizations, USAID strengthens their ability to advocate and engage with government officials to deliver quality social services.
- The Department also is running a project in Nigeria to educate civil society, extractive industry leaders, and government officials about human rights and promote the incorporation of the Voluntary Principles on Security and Human Rights, which apply to the extractive sector.
- In the runup to Nigeria's February 2015 elections, the United States is reinforcing the electoral process through support to the Independent National Electoral Commission (INEC) and political parties. We also continue to stress our concerns to INEC and the Nigerian Government that any suspension of democratic or electoral processes in northeastern Nigeria could undermine the integrity of the elections.
- USAID also facilitates dialogue among government institutions, civil society, political parties, faith-based organizations, and other stakeholders to prevent, manage, and mitigate the impact of conflict, including election-related conflict.

All these initiatives are part of a coordinated effort to help strengthen Nigeria's ability to respond responsibly and effectively to these challenges in a way that ensures civilians are protected and human rights are respected.

Question. According to the State Department, corruption in Nigeria is "massive, widespread and pervasive."

♦ How have allegations of corruption and lack of transparency affected civilians views of the Nigerian Government?
♦ Has this led to distrust and/or animosity?
♦ How does this corruption impact our relationship with the Nigerian Government?

Answer. Pervasive corruption remains a central impediment to effective governance, economic development and stability in Nigeria. Public demands for meaningful reforms and an end to impunity for corrupt officials have grown over the past year, to include an ongoing campaign to pressure President Jonathan to publically declare his personal assets. Nigerians consistently view their public institutions as corrupt and cite the police and national government officials as the most corrupt. This perception fuels public distrust in government institutions. For example, reliable polling conducted in 2013 illustrated that 85 percent of Nigerians believe there is at least a fair amount of corruption among the police and as a result only 23 percent of the public trust the police. The Nigerian military is not immune to the Nigeria's broader corruption challenges, and corruption within the military erodes the effectiveness of security forces engaged in combating Boko Haram.

To reduce the culture of impunity for those who engage in corruption, we support Nigerian anticorruption agencies, such as the Economic and Financial Crimes Commission, to develop the capacity to investigate and prosecute cases relating to high-level corruption or financial crime. We are also working with civil society to advance transparent and accountable governance. In 2013, the State Department launched a 2-year pilot program that will build the capacity of civil society (including media) to work with government agencies to fight corruption and transnational organized crime by leveraging citizens' access to government-held information. We also continue to promote anticorruption and human rights norms through engagement with high-level officials from the Nigerian Police Force on the subject of restarting bilateral police training. In 2006 we had to end trainings after the former Inspector General of Police was convicted of stealing $83 million from the Police Force.

Question. Amnesty International has reported that thousands of people suspected of links to Boko Haram have been extrajudicially executed or unlawfully killed by security forces, and thousands of suspects have died in military or police custody.

♦ How have these abuses fueled the conflict and how do they constrain our ability to help the Nigerian Government respond to this crisis?

Answer. Boko Haram has carried out a brutal campaign of terror that has killed over 1,500 innocent civilians since the beginning of the year. It has attacked churches, mosques and schools, burned villages, killed political official and security officers, and kidnapped innocent children. Unfortunately, the Nigerian security forces have responded to this brutality with their own heavy-handed tactics. These tactics have involved human rights violations that include extrajudicial killings and prisoner deaths. The continued lack of accountability for these violations has reinforced preexisting perceptions of many northerners that the Nigerian Government does not care about them. This situation can compromise the credibility of those international partners who attempt to help the Government of Nigeria address the legitimate need to combat violent extremism if the partners are perceived as condoning or overlooking the heavy-handed tactics of the Nigerian security forces. In turn, criminal terrorist groups such as Boko Haram use these circumstances to exploit the grievances of the northern population to garner recruits and public support.

Consequently, the United States continues to encourage the Government of Nigeria to implement a comprehensive approach to combating Boko Haram that addresses the underlying causes of the conflict and grievances of northern populations while at the same time emphasizing civilian protection, respect for human rights, the rule of law, and accountable security forces. Defeating Boko Haram requires much more than a military response; it also requires coordination among civilian law enforcement entities, civic and political outreach, and development that addresses the legitimate concerns of the people of northern Nigeria.

RESPONSE OF EARL GAST AND AMBASSADOR ROBERT P. JACKSON TO QUESTION SUBMITTED BY SENATOR BENJAMIN L. CARDIN

Question. There are girls in Nigeria and around the world risking their lives every day to get an education—it is time for the administration to stand behind them in the long term. Under Goal 3 of the Education Strategy, USAID has pledged to expand access to education for children and youth living in conflict and crisis situations. Currently there are more than 57 million primary school-aged children who are not in school worldwide and half of them live in countries affected by armed conflict.

♦ Will the U.S. step up its leadership role by significantly increasing support for the Global Partnership for Education (GPE) replenishment conference in June?
♦ What steps can the U.S. take to promote better and safer access to education in Nigeria, particularly in the North?

Answer. USAID will participate in the GPE replenishment conference at the end of June. USAID is currently in the process of planning its budget for the release of FY 2014 funds, and the U.S. contribution to the GPE is part of that budget strategy. While we anticipate that the FY 2014 contribution to the GPE will increase, final determinations on FY 2014 allocations have not yet been made. We would be happy to follow up with you and/or your staff once the amount in FY 2014 allocations are finalized.

USAID currently focuses the vast majority of education program resources for Nigeria in the northern region of the country, where national education indicators are the lowest. USAID is coordinating education activities in northern Nigeria with the United Kingdom's Department for International Development (DFID), to ensure the maximum impact and geographical coverage. Additionally, USAID is developing a new program that will specifically address equitable access to quality education in the areas that are affected by conflict and safety concerns. Last, it is important to note that USAID has some education related programs that are not in the north. These programs support nationwide household and schooling data collection and a national children's television program.

———

RESPONSES OF AMBASSADOR ROBERT JACKSON TO QUESTIONS
SUBMITTED BY SENATOR ROBERT MENENDEZ

Question. Human Rights Abuses by Nigerian Military.—Despite Nigeria's strategic importance as Africa's most populous nation and largest economy, our security assistance has historically been constrained by human rights abuses committed by Nigerian soldiers in their campaign against Boko Haram. These have been well documented in, for example, the State Department's 2013 Human Rights Report.

◆ How are we working with the government to correct this troubling record in order to ensure that the Nigerian people have a military they can trust and that the international community has a stable security partner moving forward? What accountability measures are we pushing the Nigerian Government to implement?

Answer. The United States has been very open about our concerns about Nigeria's human rights record. We continue to encourage the Government of Nigeria to implement a comprehensive approach to combating Boko Haram that addresses the underlying causes of conflict and valid grievances of northern populations while emphasizing civilian protection, respect for human rights, rule of law, and accountability of security forces. We ensure that promoting respect for human rights is a key aspect of any assistance we provide to Nigerian security forces.

We have urged the Government of Nigeria to work with the families of victims and their communities in order to bring to justice not only those responsible for acts of terrorism, but also Nigerian security officials responsible for unlawful violence and abuses against civilian populations, including detainees. Impartial accountability for serious crimes committed by all sides is necessary to break the cycle of violence. We continue to push the Government of Nigeria to take steps to ensure accountability for security forces by conducting credible investigations and prosecuting the individuals responsible.

Question. U.S. Efforts to Address the Boko Haram Threat.—I hope this is the last time we have a conversation about such a horrific event at the hands of Boko Haram, but, realistically, it probably won't be. The chaos and brutality perpetrated by Boko Haram is not isolated to this incident and is increasing.

◆ Does the changing nature of the threat put U.S. interests at additional risk?
◆ Of our significant bilateral assistance (some $700 million), a relatively small portion (an estimated $10–20 million) is devoted to counterterrorism efforts—is this adequate?

Answer. To date, Boko Haram has not specifically targeted U.S. citizens in its attacks. However, in his public statements Boko Haram's leader, Abubakar Shekau, has threatened to attack U.S. interests, and we remain concerned about the growing threat to our interests in the region as Boko Haram expands the geographic scope of its operations. The U.S. mission in Nigeria monitors closely any such threats to official and private American citizens and their interests, and provides guidance accordingly.

The administration continues to encourage the Nigerian Government to implement a comprehensive approach toward combating violent extremism and insecurity in northeastern Nigeria, which stresses addressing legitimate grievances of northern populations. As a result, the majority of our bilateral assistance focuses on the Nigerian population's most serious grievances. These include unemployment, infrastructure, sanitation, health care, education, political marginalization, and corruption.

Additionally, Nigeria benefits from centrally managed assistance through programs such as the Trans Sahara Counterterrorism Partnership (TSCTP) and the West Africa Regional Security Initiative (WARSI), which are not reflected in the country's bilateral funding levels.

Our current levels of security assistance devoted to counter terrorism in Nigeria are appropriate, contingent upon the Nigerian Government's ability to absorb the assistance, emphasize civilian protection, respect human rights and the rule of law, and develop accountable security forces.

Question. Support to Civil Society.—A security-centric approach has led to an out-of-control insurgency and repeated human rights abuses in the Middle East, Mali, and elsewhere. And yet, since the abductions, the international community has been primarily focused on security assistance to the Nigerian Government.

♦ How is the United States supporting local civil society organizations, including local and international interreligious and peace-building organizations, to ensure a balanced, well-rounded approach to protect civilians and prevent Boko Haram from becoming even more emboldened?

Answer. The U.S. Embassy supports local religious leaders who reach across sectarian lines and promote human rights, social justice, and conflict resolution. USAID has conducted conflict mitigation and management interventions to lessen sectarian and intercommunal tensions and to increase interfaith civic engagement and tolerance among flashpoint communities.

In May 2014, the U.S. Special Envoy to the Organization of Islamic Cooperation (OIC) held a series of video conferences with leading Nigerian Islamic leaders representing a wide range of Muslim communities in Nigeria to discuss strategies for countering Boko Haram's narrative. USAID is also providing training to religious and traditional leaders to help increase stability in Nigeria by enhancing the legitimacy and capacity of governance structures to defend religious freedom.

USAID is helping to strengthen education management systems; improve the reading skills of 5.5 million northern Nigerian primary school students; improve the quality of education for teachers to teach reading, and increase access of orphans and vulnerable children, including itinerant Qur'anic youth (Almajiri), and girls, to basic education. These programs focus on the northern states of Bauchi and Sokoto.

The United States is working with civil society to advance transparent and accountable governance. In 2013, the State Department launched a 2-year pilot program to build the capacity of civil society (including media) to increase citizens' access to government-held information. The State Department also is running a project in Nigeria to educate civil society, extractive industry leaders, and government officials about human rights and promote the incorporation of the Voluntary Principles on Security and Human Rights, which apply to the extractive sector. Through a pilot program in the Niger Delta, the State Department is working with civil society organizations to enhance nonviolent problem-solving between communities and government through a multimedia campaign and targeted assistance. The engagement counters the narrative that violence is the only effective means to create change. USAID also works with civil society to strengthen its ability to influence the development and implementation of key democratic reforms at national, state, and local levels.

The Embassy in Abuja is about to launch a portfolio of activities totaling $1.7 million targeting northern, at-risk youth. These projects will be implemented through the public affairs and political sections, and will build upon a new multiyear Hausa language satellite television initiative (Arewa 24) and ongoing VOA radio programming. These youth-oriented projects will transmit information on job skills as well as entrepreneurial and employment opportunities, and will address concepts of cultural tolerance and communication. The Embassy is working through local NGOs to address the scourge of children pressed into street begging. Our efforts support ongoing local stakeholder efforts to stamp out these abuses that too often result in children (the so-called ''al-majiri'') being vulnerable to recruitment into violent gangs and networks as they get older, including Boko Haram.

All these initiatives are part of a coordinated effort to strengthen Nigeria's ability to respond responsibly and effectively to these challenges in a way that ensures civilians are protected and human rights are respected.

––––––––––

RESPONSES OF AMBASSADOR ROBERT JACKSON TO QUESTIONS
SUBMITTED BY SENATOR BOB CORKER

Question. 1. The administration has provided numerous assessments of Boko Haram's threat as limited to Nigeria and an occasional regional outreach as was seen recently in its involvement in Mali and ongoing safe haven and sporadic violence in neighboring Niger, Chad, and Cameroon. Nonetheless, internally it has become more sophisticated and lethal with over 1,500 Nigerians killed since the first of the year, hundreds of children and others abducted for ransom and trafficking, and the recent threat to western hotels in Abuja.

♦ Even though Boko Haram's place in the global threat matrix might appear less relevant to the U.S. given its limited reach beyond Nigeria, should the United

States take a more strategic approach to limiting its further influence in the face of this mounting capacity to destabilize a large regional power?

♦ Given the Nigerian Government's lack of capacity and political willingness to engage Boko Haram and its own reluctance to effectively cooperate with international partners, what have we learned that would improve the U.S. pursuit of its interests in the region?
♦ What practical limitations exist to U.S. cooperation with Nigeria?
♦ Please provide the waivers and exceptions to legal limitations that are permitted and how they are determined to be utilized.
♦ Have any waivers or exceptions been utilized as it relates to security cooperation with Nigeria? Have any waivers or exceptions been utilized as it relates to security cooperation with any countries in Africa?

Answer. The United States continues to reiterate privately and publically to Nigeria that we will do all we can to support the Nigerian Government to meet its responsibility for the safety and security of its own citizens. We are urging the Nigerian Government to ensure that it brings all resources to bear in a concerted, effective, and responsible effort to ensure the safe return of the abductees. The United States continues to encourage the Government of Nigeria to implement a comprehensive approach to combating Boko Haram, which addresses grievances of northern populations, and emphasizes civilian protection, respect for human rights, the rule of law, and the accountability of security forces. The United States has been open about our concerns regarding Nigeria's human rights record. We must ensure that promoting respect for human rights remains a key aspect of any assistance we provide to Nigerian security forces. Unless action is taken to severely reduce Boko Haram's capabilities, it will carry out more atrocities. At a minimum, we must work with Nigeria's neighbors and partners to prevent Boko Haram from continuing to threaten peace and security in the region.

On Leahy restrictions, the Department understands that the only possibility of resuming assistance to a unit once credible allegations of a gross violation of human rights are identified is for the host government to take effective steps to bring the responsible parties to justice. The Leahy law affecting the Department of State does not include any ability to waive Leahy restrictions. The Leahy law affecting the Department of Defense includes certain waiver provisions; we would refer you to the Department of Defense for more information.

We have not yet exercised any waivers or exceptions in fiscal year 2014 for Nigeria related to security cooperation under State Department authorities, nor have we determined yet that the immediate circumstances would warrant such action.

Assistance to other countries in Africa is subject to a number of restrictions; these restrictions include both country-specific restrictions as well as restrictions triggered by a failure to meet certain statutory standards. Fiscal year waivers for the latter category include the following:

- The Department applied restrictions under the Trafficking Victims Protection Act (TVPA) in fiscal year 2014 to the Central African Republic (CAR), Democratic Republic of the Congo (DRC), Equatorial Guinea, Eritrea, Guinea Bissau, Mauritania, Sudan, and Zimbabwe. Full waivers of these restrictions were granted to CAR, Guinea-Bissau, and Mauritania, while partial waivers were granted to the others. The restrictions were not waived for Equatorial Guinea, Eritrea, or Zimbabwe.
- The Department applied restrictions under the Child Soldier Protection Act (CSPA) in fiscal year 2014 to CAR, Chad, DRC, Rwanda, Somalia, South Sudan, and Sudan. Full waivers of these restrictions were granted to Chad and South Sudan. Partial waivers of restrictions on security assistance were granted to DRC and Somalia. No waivers were granted to CAR, Rwanda or Sudan.

Question. Direct cooperation on security with Nigeria and its neighbors encompasses a variety of programs and sources but little clarity on the coherence across or even within U.S. agencies. Testimony provided at the hearing intimated at a fairly robust cooperation in CT which appears less than apparent from funding and program reviews.

♦ Provide information on the broader U.S. security cooperation with Nigeria since 2009 and outline more recent changes and the funding sources that will be utilized, to include training or equipping, mentoring, technical assistance or other program that provides for:
  Æ Intelligence sharing;
  Æ Training to a new unit known as the 143rd Ranger Battalion;
  Æ Training to the 101st CT battalion and the 111th Special Operations Group;

Æ C–IED training and civ-mil training;
Æ Nigerian Army Special Operations Command (NASOC);
Æ And remaining GSCF funding or its replacement.

♦ Incorporate regional training and equipping programming and plans into the above strategic approach to helping Nigeria and the broader region counter militant extremists, including to provide training to the Multi-National Joint Task Force (Chad, Cameroon, Niger, and Nigeria).

♦ What if any additional outcomes emerged from the summit of heads of state that was convened by President Hollande in France on May 17 regarding the region.

Answer. The Department of State uses bilateral and regional funding from the following foreign assistance accounts to advance U.S. security cooperation with Nigeria: (1) Foreign Military Financing (FMF); (2) International Military Education and Training (IMET); (3) Peacekeeping Operations (PKO); (4) International Narcotics Control and Law Enforcement (INCLE); and (5) Nonproliferation, Antiterrorism, Demining and Related Programs (NADR).

Since 2009, Nigeria has received FMF, IMET, and/or PKO funding for enhancing capabilities for counterterrorism, peacekeeping, maritime security, and/or professionalism. Nigeria has also consistently received INCLE and NADR funding to strengthen the professionalism and capacity of select law enforcement and judicial entities, with a focus on countering terrorism and combating financial crimes. The Department of Defense also uses title 10 authorities (e.g., section 1206) to enhance cooperation with the Nigerian military.

In the face of the growing threat posed by Boko Haram, we are seeking to increase several lines of security assistance to help Nigeria pursue a more comprehensive approach toward the Boko Haram threat. For example, we have obligated $4.5 million of FY 2014 PKO funding allocated as part of the Trans-Sahara Counterterrorism Partnership (TSCTP) to build Nigerian military capabilities for civil-military operations and countering improvised explosive devices. We are also planning to increase FY 2014 NADR funding allocated to TSCTP to expand Antiterrorism Assistance (ATA) training for Nigerian law enforcement agencies. Separately, we are using prior year FMF funding obligated for Nigeria to support U.S. training of Nigeria's 143rd Ranger Battalion and possibly other vetted units of the Nigerian military.

In addition to building Nigeria's counterterrorism capabilities, we continue to promote enhanced regional cooperation and capacity to counter the Boko Haram threat. We are encouraging Cameroon, Chad, Niger, and Nigeria to follow through on their commitments to establish a regional task force to combat Boko Haram, building on regional mechanisms such as the Multinational Joint Task Force for Lake Chad (MNJTF). We will seek to support these efforts as much as possible. Through TSCTP, we continue to provide a range of bilateral and regional assistance to Niger and Chad to enhance their counterterrorism capabilities. We added Cameroon as a member of TSCTP earlier this year, which will enable its participation in this programming. In addition, State and DOD are finalizing a plan for a proposed $40 million program to help the governments of Cameroon, Chad, Niger, and Nigeria develop institutional and tactical capabilities to enhance joint efforts to counter Boko Haram and to lay the groundwork for increased cross-border cooperation to counter Boko Haram.

As a result of the May 17 summit in Paris, Nigeria and its neighbors agreed to do the following, with international assistance:

• Implement coordinated patrols with the aim of combating Boko Haram and locating the missing school girls;
• Establish a system to pool intelligence in order to support this operation;
• Establish mechanisms for information exchange on trafficking of weapons and bolster measures to secure weapons stockpiles;
• Establish mechanisms for border surveillance;
• Establish an intelligence pooling unit; and
• Create a dedicated team to identify means of implementation and draw up, during a second phase, a regional counterterrorism strategy.

Nigeria's neighbors and friends in the international community have maintained a strong, united resolve in helping Nigeria and its neighbors combat and defeat violent extremism. We are committed to a comprehensive, long-term approach, while also working to see the kidnapped girls return home safely.

Question. The continuing challenge for the United States is that our efforts will have to be creative and coordinated, not only with a partner in Nigeria who is reluctant to do so, but with regional neighbors who have much to lose if this violent militancy spreads, as reports indicate it can.

♦ What is the state of U.S. cooperation with neighbors in Niger, Chad, and Cameroon and set it against the domestic capacity of these three countries to address the border security threat as well as the respective governments efforts to address internal tensions that may mirror Nigeria's current situation?

♦ How have we utilized the Trans-Sahara Counter-Terrorism Partnership and other Countering Violent Extremism and other CT programs in the region to address the growing Boko Haram threat and how are they to be augmented if at all? What office or vehicle for coordination exists to harmonize such regionally significant programs as CT–CVE?

Answer. As a result of the May 17 regional summit in Paris, Nigeria and its neighbors agreed to do the following, with international assistance:

- Implement coordinated patrols with the aim of combating Boko Haram and locating the missing school girls;
- Establish a system to pool intelligence in order to support this operation;
- Establish mechanisms for information exchange on trafficking of weapons and bolster measures to secure weapons stockpiles;
- Establish mechanisms for border surveillance;
- Establish an intelligence pooling unit; and
- Create a dedicated team to identify means of implementation and draw up, during a second phase, a regional counterterrorism strategy.

With support from the Government of France, Nigeria has recently attempted to establish border security cooperation agreements with its neighbors and to strengthen the Multinational Joint Task Force for Lake Chad (MNJTF). However, actual cross-border cooperation remains ad hoc. Alongside the French, the United Kingdom, and other international partners, we are working to encourage the development of stronger regional mechanisms to counter Boko Haram and other cross-border threats. We are also developing new programs to assist Nigeria, Niger, Chad, and Cameroon to develop enhanced border security capabilities (e.g., command-and-control, communications, logistics, and tactical reconnaissance). All four countries need significant assistance in developing these capabilities.

Through the Trans-Sahara Counterterrorism Partnership (TSCTP), the United States seeks to build the capacity and resilience of military, law enforcement, and civilian actors across the Sahel and Maghreb regions to counter terrorist groups, including Boko Haram. The State Department's Bureau of African Affairs oversees TSCTP and chairs an interagency working group to align programs and strategies. Chad, Niger, and Nigeria are longstanding TSCTP partners and have benefited from various TSCTP's programs. Earlier this year, the United States added Cameroon as a TSCTP partner nation, which will enable it to participate in future TSCTP programming.

The Department's Bureau of Counterterrorism oversees a variety of programs to help defeat Boko Haram (and Ansaru) under the framework of TSCTP. Through the Antiterrorism Assistance (ATA) program, the Department trains law enforcement in Nigeria, Chad, Niger, and soon in Cameroon, to counter the threat posed by Boko Haram and effectively respond to and manage terrorist attacks. ATA training and associated equipment grants build the capacity of police, Gendarme, and other law enforcement CT-focused units on border security, investigations (including post-blast investigations), and critical incident management.

Our Countering Violent Extremism (CVE) programs aim to limit recruits to Boko Haram by reducing sympathy and support for its operations, through three primary objectives: (1) building resilience among communities most at risk of recruitment and radicalization to violence; (2) countering Boko Haram narratives and messaging; and (3) building the CVE capacity of government and civil society. Such efforts include promoting engagement between law enforcement and citizens, and elevating the role of women civil society leaders in CVE.

These efforts include USAID support to promote conflict mitigation and reconciliation programs in six Nigerian states. Further, the Public Affairs Section at U.S. Embassy in Abuja and USAID work with northern Nigerian youth, women through mass media education programs with countering violent extremism messaging. USAID and Centers for Disease Control (CDC) programs focus on development of health, agricultural, and educational programs in nearly all states of Northern Nigeria. The Bureau of Counterterrorism and Center for Strategic Counterterrorism Communications (CSCC) have developed a strong partnership with the Office of the National Security Adviser (ONSA)'s Strategic Communications/CVE office and, in conjunction with the United Kingdom, provided assistance on developing a comprehensive communications strategy.

USAID's current TSCTP activities include a regional Peace for Development (PDEV II) program in Burkina Faso, Niger, and Chad. PDEV II is a 5-year $60 million initiative launched in November 2011 that applies a holistic, community-led approach. PDEV II covers a large number of geographically distant and often culturally, linguistically, and socioeconomically diverse communities. Given the immensity of the Sahel, interventions are limited to communities with the highest violent extremism risk factors, determined through assessments conducted by the project. A number of those target communities are in areas of both Niger and Chad that border Nigeria. To date, nearly 3.8 million people from at-risk groups have been reached through various USAID PDEV II activities, including youth-led community mobilization activities; radio programming; and training in management skills, budgeting, leadership, vocational trades, and conflict resolution.

We also work closely with Nigeria within the Global Counterterrorism Forum (GCTF) framework—an informal, multilateral counterterrorism (CT) platform that focuses on identifying critical civilian CT needs, mobilizing the necessary expertise and resources to address such needs and enhance global cooperation. As one of the member states of the GCTF, Nigeria has cohosted with us several regional workshops focusing on human rights and law enforcement issues. Nigeria has also agreed to become a pilot country to the Global Community Engagement and Resilience Fund (GCERF), a GCTF-inspired initiative announced by Secretary Kerry at the September 2013 GCTF ministerial. This will enable community-based organizations in Nigeria to receive grants from the GCERF to carry out grassroots CVE projects. Furthermore, Nigeria will be one of the founding members of the International Institute for Justice and the Rule of Law in Malta, whose primary mission will be to train justice and security sector officials on how to prevent and respond to terrorist activity and other transnational criminal activity within a rule of law framework.

———

RESPONSES OF EARL GAST TO QUESTIONS
SUBMITTED BY SENATOR ROBERT MENENDEZ

HUMANITARIAN AND DEVELOPMENT ASSISTANCE IN THE NORTH

I am particularly interested in U.S. efforts in the isolated northeast, where there is an ongoing state of emergency and where development indicators are especially concerning and have contributed to a sense of alienation.

Question. What specific efforts are underway to support the people of Nigeria to overcome key social and economic drivers of instability, such as entrenched poverty, corruption, displacement, ethnic and religious strife, and poor service delivery?

Answer. USAID programming in northern Nigeria is designed to help the Government of Nigeria (GON) address sources of disenfranchisement by improving its ability to promote private-sector-led economic growth and provide basic services to its citizens. The USAID portfolio in the north is comprehensive, ranging from agriculture to health to education to governance. Several large projects are geographically colocated in the states of Bauchi and Sokoto—states with heightened developmental need—in an effort to maximize developmental impact. It is important to note that USAID is currently implementing activities in states adjacent to the "State of Emergency" states—states which are receiving significant numbers of internally displaced persons who place additional stress on already weak social service provision. Expansion of USAID programming into State of Emergency states would depend entirely on the security situation.

In addition to the following programs in northern Nigeria, USAID is currently carrying out an assessment of all mission programs and activities to improve understanding of the drivers and mitigating factors of armed conflict in Nigeria, ensure all USAID programming minimizes the risk of exacerbating conflict dynamics, and to the degree possible, mitigates drivers of conflict over issues that intersect with sectors such as health, education, and agriculture.

Democracy and Governance

USAID works with state and local governments to improve budget preparation and fiscal oversight to ensure adequate service delivery. Working with a diverse group of civil society organizations, USAID strengthens their ability to advocate and engage with government officials to deliver quality social services. USAID also facilitates dialogue among government institutions, civil society, political parties, faith-based organizations, and other stakeholders to prevent, manage, and mitigate the impact of conflict.

Health and HIV/AIDS

USAID supports increased access to quality family planning and reproductive health services, immunization and polio eradication, and maternal health services. USAID also supports efforts to decrease the number of malaria-related deaths in pregnant women and children each year by increasing access to and availability of treatment, insecticide-treated bed nets, and retreatment kits. USAID provides HIV/AIDS prevention, care and treatment services, as well as services to orphans and vulnerable children. Detection and treatment services for tuberculosis are also provided.

Education

USAID provides technical assistance at all levels of government in the two northern Nigerian states of Bauchi and Sokoto to ensure that the human and financial resources are available and mobilized for the education sector. USAID programs support equitable access to quality basic education through teacher training, support for girls' learning, infrastructure improvement, community involvement, and reading and literacy skills development. The programs target public schools, as well as Islamiyyah schools, which provide both secular and religious education.

Economic Growth

USAID supports Nigeria's poverty alleviation efforts by improving agricultural productivity and expanding jobs in the rural sector. USAID's program supports market-based solutions and privatization of the energy sector for improved efficiency. Additionally, USAID helps to improve access to safe drinking water and reduce morbidity and mortality due to water-borne and sanitation-related illnesses.

Question. What kind of humanitarian and development programming is possible to both assist Nigerians and counter Boko Haram's false and inflammatory rhetoric that the United States is at war with Islam?

Answer. In mid-2013, USAID commissioned an assessment of violent extremism in Nigeria. The study provides the underlying historical, economic, political, and cultural forces that led to the formation of Boko Haram. Due to the high level of instability in the most affected states, as well as the complexity of the Government of Nigeria response, the assessment recommends development assistance interventions that indirectly counter violent extremism by enhancing economic opportunity for young men in the agricultural sector or improving the curriculum and education options offered at semiformal Koranic schools. This report was shared with USAID's counterparts in the Government of Nigeria formulating a development component to their counterterrorism strategy.

The Office of Transition Initiatives (OTI) has also sent a team to assess the situation in northeastern Nigeria as it relates to political instability, violence, and lawlessness brought about by the growing threat of Boko Haram throughout the region. This assessment will provide OTI with a better understanding of the situation and its effect on political stability in the region, allow OTI, USAID/Nigeria, and the interagency to consider holistic approaches for a coherent and comprehensive response to Boko Haram-related issues, and consider the feasibility of any programming recommendations given security conditions in the target region.

Question. We have heard that USAID is planning to move OFDA money to address needs in the northeast region of Nigeria. Could you please provide more details on the types of projects those funds will support?

Answer. The Office of U.S. Foreign Disaster Assistance (OFDA) is working with other donors to determine the humanitarian needs of those affected by this crisis. OFDA has already provided $100,000 to support trauma counseling and psychosocial assistance in Borno State for the abducted girls upon their return as well as for their families. USAID/OFDA has also committed $750,000 to the International Organization for Migration to improve the timely tracking and monitoring of internally displaced persons and humanitarian needs in conflict affected areas, which will help improve the delivery of critical, appropriate humanitarian assistance for affected populations. OFDA expects to provide additional humanitarian assistance that will target internally displaced people and their host communities. Anticipated humanitarian needs include: food and nonfood items, food security, protection/psychosocial support, livelihoods, shelter, emergency education, livelihoods, water, sanitation, and hygiene.

Within the last several months, OFDA staff has traveled to Gombe, Bauchi, and Adamawa states, and has a strong understanding of the humanitarian needs in those areas. To date, support to those affected by the conflict has been hindered due to the increase in frequency of violent attacks in 2014. Currently, humanitarian access is possible, albeit precarious due to the volatile nature of the security threat.

Responses of Earl Gast to Questions
Submitted by Senator Christopher A. Coons

Question. Electricity.—Since towns such as Chibok have limited to no electricity, what is USAID doing to bring electricity to the North? Obviously, Nigeria is one of the six Power Africa focus countries. Are there any Power Africa projects in the North, and what more could we do to partner with the Nigerian Government to address energy poverty?

Answer. The Government of Nigeria, and in particular, the Ministry of Power, has prioritized expanding electricity access in the North through renewable and other approaches. The Nigerian Bulk Electricity Trader (NBET) had presented the North Solar Capital Project as one of their priority efforts. There are significant challenges with this project due to security issues and the ability of private investors and financial institutions to effectively carry out due diligence and monitor the project.

The Minister of Power, Mr. Chinedu Nebo, has approached USAID and other donors with ideas on how to support off grid and mini-grid projects in the North as part of a nationwide effort to bring access through off-grid and mini-grid projects to areas that lack access. Working with other donors, USAID can potentially look at what incentives and risk mitigation measures can be put into place to encourage development of projects in the North, but it will be a complex and challenging process. USAID and the Power Africa team are also providing technical advice to renewable energy project developers on how to navigate the various government agencies while developing bankable and sound proposals.

Question. Education.—Given that children are risking their lives to go to school because education is so important, can you address the administration's decision to cut funding for international basic education programs by 33 percent from the current levels?

Answer. In response to the very robust appropriation for education funding in FY 2013, the Nigeria education program received a 24-percent increase in funds above their prior year levels. However, because of the fragile security environment and difficulties in operating in northern Nigeria where education funds are needed most, USAID adjusted some activities and temporarily drew down its work pending a change in the security environment. Currently, USAID is addressing this by pursuing new programming options which specifically focus on increasing access to education and improving reading performance through institutional strengthening activities. In response to the major increase in FY 2013 education funds, and to ensure that the Nigeria program has the resources it requires to sustain other critical investments, including democracy and governance programs, the Agency proposed a lower level of education funding for Nigeria in FY 2014. That level increases in the FY 2015 request by 15 percent as the prior year education funds on hand are drawn down.

Response of Alice Friend to Question
Submitted by Senator Christopher A. Coons

Question. Professionalization of the Military.—It has been mentioned that U.S. support for the professionalization of Nigeria's military has been ongoing. What improvements have you seen as a result of that support? Since professionalization of the military is so important to addressing Boko Haram, why is the FY15 request for Foreign Military Financing (FMF) for Nigerian $400,000 less than it was in FY14?

Answer. Promoting professionalization among foreign militaries is a long-term, even generational, process. In the case of Nigeria, DOD believes that our progress to date manifests itself in two distinct ways. The first is the deliberate and ongoing effort to provide Nigerian officers, noncommissioned officers, and other military personnel examples of what military professionals look like and how they conduct themselves. We consider every training event, exercise, and day-to-day interaction to be a powerful and important opportunity to influence and shape the behavior of Nigeria's military. Second, under the Africa Military Education Program (AMEP), DOD is supporting Nigerian efforts to overhaul and expand the curricula at two of its professional military education institutions. Once complete, this initiative will provide Nigeria with its own organic capability to promote a more professional officer corps across its armed forces, now and into the future. Foreign Military Financing (FMF) levels alone are an insufficient metric to gauge DOD's resolve or commitment to helping Nigeria professionalize its military. A wide range of other authorities and funding sources are brought to bear to address the professionalization challenge, including International Military Education and Training (IMET) and section 1206 authorities, for example.

RESPONSES OF ALICE FRIEND TO QUESTIONS
SUBMITTED BY SENATOR BENJAMIN L. CARDIN

Question. Extrajudicial Executions and Unlawful Killings by Security Forces.— Amnesty International has reported that thousands of people suspected of links to Boko Haram have been extrajudicially executed or unlawfully killed by security forces, and thousands of suspects have died in military or police custody.

◆ How have these abuses fueled the conflict and how do they constrain our ability to help the Nigerian Government respond to this crisis?

Answer. The reported abuses committed by Nigeria's security forces actively feed the very extremist ideology Nigeria is attempting to defeat, and thus undermine its counterinsurgency efforts. Moreover, such abuses trigger provisions of U.S. domestic law that preclude the United States from providing assistance and training to units about which there is credible information that a member of the unit has committed a gross violation of human rights. As a result, we are limited in our ability to help develop the expertise, skills, and abilities Nigeria lacks and that are indispensable to its success against Boko Haram. A significant percentage of Nigeria's Army, including the 7th Division, which has been assigned to northeast Nigeria to conduct counter-Boko Haram operations, is excluded from U.S. counterterrorism (CT) capacity-building assistance due to its failure to be successfully vetted under the DOD "Leahy law." The Nigerian Special Boat Service has been a notable exception and has been successfully vetted, as there is no credible information that this unit has committed gross violations of human rights. Similarly, a newly created Nigerian "Ranger Battalion" has been successfully vetted, and U.S. Africa Command personnel are currently conducting training on basic individual and unit military skills.

Question. Long-Term U.S. Strategy.—What is the long-term U.S. strategy for countering Boko Haram in Nigeria? In your opinion, how receptive is Nigeria to U.S. technical assistance? How much can we really do within the confines of our laws?

Answer. U.S. Africa Command forces are presently laying the groundwork for a regional, partner force-led counterterrorism effort in Nigeria, Cameroon, Niger, and Chad that focuses on border security. Continued congressional support for various uncodified National Defense Authorization Act (NDAA) provisions authorizing DOD support to foreign forces is critical to the success of this effort. The U.S. strategy is to promote a Nigerian whole-of-government approach that addresses the full range of social, economic, governance, security, and other factors that contribute to Nigeria's instability and insecurity, particularly in the north. We have consistently advised the Government of Nigeria that although security capacity-building is an indispensable element of its counter-Boko Haram efforts, a force-centric approach that fails to address legitimate northern Nigerian grievances will ultimately be unsuccessful. The receptivity of Nigeria's military to U.S. assistance varies within its Navy and Air Force, with some elements being more receptive to train-and-equip efforts than others. The Nigerian military's well-documented record of human rights abuses has rendered approximately 50 percent of its army "off limits" for purposes of U.S. train-and-equip efforts. We do engage and will continue to engage with those units that have been successfully vetted for human rights abuses, including its Special Boat Service and, most recently, the 143rd Infantry Battalion.

RESPONSES OF ALICE FRIEND TO QUESTIONS SUBMITTED BY SENATOR BOB CORKER

Question. Threat Assessment.—The administration has provided numerous assessments of Boko Haram's threat as limited to Nigeria and an occasional regional outreach as was seen recently in its involvement in Mali and ongoing safe haven and sporadic violence in neighboring Niger, Chad, and Cameroon. Nonetheless, internally it has become more sophisticated and lethal with over 1,500 Nigerians killed since the first of the year, hundreds of children and others abducted for ransom and trafficking, and the recent threat to Western hotels in Abuja.

◆ Even though Boko Haram's place in the global threat matrix might appear less relevant to the U.S. given its limited reach beyond Nigeria, should the United States take a more strategic approach to limiting its further influence in the face of this mounting capacity to destabilize a large regional power?

◆ Given the Nigerian Government's lack of capacity and political willingness to engage Boko Haram and its own reluctance to effectively cooperate with international partners, what have we learned that would improve the U.S. pursuit of its interests in the region?

♦ What practical limitations exist to U.S. cooperation with Nigeria?

♦ Please provide the waivers and exceptions to legal limitations that are permitted and how they are determined to be utilized.

♦ Have any waivers or exceptions been utilized as it relates to security cooperation with Nigeria? Have any waivers or exceptions been utilized as it relates to security cooperation with any countries in Africa?

Answer. Although it has only come to the public's notice since the tragic kidnapping of school girls from Chibok, DOD has recognized the relevance and growing threat of Boko Haram since 2009 when it reemerged in a new and more lethal form after going dormant for several years. Indeed, in June 2012, then-commander of U.S. Africa Command General Carter Ham, described Boko Haram as one of the three most dangerous groups operating in Africa.

Moreover, Boko Haram's transnational nature and linkages have long been recognized and known to be growing. As it has grown as a regional threat and as Nigeria's limitations in combating the group have become clearer, we have adjusted our engagement efforts accordingly. As a practical example, DOD and the Department of State have collaborated to develop a $40M package using the Global Security Contingency Fund (GSCF) authority to train border security forces in Chad, Cameroon, Niger, and Nigeria, to check Boko Haram's largely unfettered movement back and forth across regional borders. We anticipate this proposal being notified to the relevant congressional committees soon, and we look forward to collaborating closely with Congress on this important initiative.

Nigeria presents the United States with a range of challenges and limitations as a counterterrorism (CT) partner. The baseline capacities of its security forces to take on the sophisticated threat Boko Haram represents was and remains extremely low. Nigeria has never faced a terrorism or insurgency threat as intense as it currently faces, and has been slow to adapt new security strategies, tactics, and doctrines to support more effective operations.

Similarly, Nigeria has failed to adopt a whole-of-government approach that takes into account the legitimate grievances of its population, particularly in the north, thereby failing to pursue an indispensable element of any successful counterinsurgency strategy. And, perhaps most debilitating, it has conducted brutal and often indiscriminate military campaigns that have victimized its own citizens; Nigeria's security forces are believed to be responsible for the deaths of nearly as many innocent civilians as Boko Haram itself. Beyond these factors, a scarcity of political will and rampant corruption at all levels and within all elements of government limit the United States ability to bring about necessary change.

DOD has not sought waivers that would permit more robust security cooperation with Nigeria and is not convinced that Nigeria is a good candidate for such waivers. Even if waivers were granted, it is not clear that the engagement opportunities that would be made available through the waiver process would produce significant improvement in Nigeria's ability to combat Boko Haram. Although Nigeria's record of human rights violations does significantly limit the units DOD is able to train and equip, the other factors noted above are at least as limiting in terms of the U.S. ability to build the necessary CT capacities.

Question. Cooperation with Nigeria.—Direct cooperation on security with Nigeria and its neighbors encompasses a variety of programs and sources but little clarity on the coherence across or even within U.S. agencies. Testimony provided at the hearing intimated at a fairly robust cooperation in CT which appears less than apparent from funding and program reviews.

♦ Provide information on the broader U.S. security cooperation with Nigeria since 2009 and outline more recent changes and the funding sources that will be utilized, to include training or equipping, mentoring, technical assistance or other program that provides for:

    Æ   Intelligence-sharing;

    Æ   Training to a new unit known as the 143d Ranger Battalion;

    Æ   Training to the 101st CT battalion and the 111th Special Operations Group;

    Æ   C–IED training and civ-mil training;

    Æ   Nigerian Army Special Operations Command (NASOC);

    Æ   And remaining GSCF funding or its replacement.

♦ Incorporate regional training and equipping programming and plans into the above strategic approach to helping Nigeria and the broader region counter militant extremists, including to provide training to the Multi-National Joint Task Force (Chad, Cameroon, Niger, and Nigeria).

♦ What if any additional outcomes emerged from the summit of heads of state that was convened by President Hollande in France on May 17 regarding the region.

Answer. *USSOCOM–SOCAF CT/COIN Lessons Learned Exchange:* From January 13–18, 2014, U.S. Special Operations Command Africa (SOCAFRICA) personnel participated in a counterterrorism/counterinsurgency (CT/COIN) seminar with Nigerian Army and Navy representatives at Wu Bassey Barracks in Abuja. The seminar discussed U.S. and Nigerian successes, mistakes, and lessons learned in CT/COIN operations during their respective campaigns against terrorism. Each topic was introduced and taught by both U.S. and Nigerian instructors, after which participants broke into workgroups to discuss the topic and how it could be interpreted and put to use in Nigeria's current situation. The CT/COIN seminar reflected upon past experiences—both positive and negative—and emphasized key lessons to be applied in future operations.

Intelligence Fusion Center: U.S. Africa Command and other DOD elements are supporting interagency efforts to develop a Nigerian National Intelligence Fusion Center (IFC) in Abuja. The IFC mission will be to synchronize efforts of Nigerian intelligence and security communities, institutionalize collaborative communications among national defense, foreign relations, CT, and law enforcement organizations, and improve Nigeria's ability to detect and preempt terrorist activities. This is a modest train-and-equip program utilizing counternarcotics funding in light of the ''narco'' nexus with Nigeria's National Drug and Law Enforcement Agency (NDLEA).

143d Infantry Battalion (INF BN): On April 23, 2014, U.S. Army Africa began a 4-week series of familiarization events with key 143 INF BN staff leading to a 5-week Foreign Military Sales (FMS)-funded field training period on individual and units tasks. The FMS portion will include communication, land navigation, squad and platoon tactics, law of armed conflict, and human rights training. Company-level training will include urban operations, cordon and search, reconnaissance, and MEDEVAC. Specialized staff training includes the military decisionmaking process, fires integration, and intelligence-driven targeting. The training period will culminate in a battalion training exercise to apply gained knowledge.

Section 1206 human rights training and equipment transfer to the 101st CT Battalion (CT BN). This $2.25M FY 2009 Section 1206 Light Infantry Company redirected from Chad to Nigeria (plus supplemental package) was originally an FY 2007 funded section 1206 program for Chad, which could not be executed. The case was redirected to Nigeria in FY 2009, but the training was postponed because of human rights concerns. Nigeria was unable to establish an acceptable national CT unit that could successfully be vetted until November 2013, with the establishment and vetting of the 101st CT BN. A Defense Institute of International Legal Studies (DIILS) team went to Abuja May 6–9, 2014, to provide Law of Armed Conflict and human rights training required in connection with this equipment transfer. The section 1206-authorized equipment (6x 8-ton trucks, 15x Land Cruisers, 2x ambulance trucks, 5x trucks, communications equipment, as well as various uniform and field equipment items) was transferred to the 101st CT BN on May 9, 2014, immediately following completion of the training.

Defense Institute of International Legal Studies (DIILS) Detainee Operations Engagement: (FOUO) DIILS, with additional engagement team support from the U.S. Army Office of the Provost Marshall General (OPMG), plans to conduct a 3–5-day Legal Aspects of Detention Operations Workshop and Exchange at the Infantry Training School Headquarters at Jaji Camp in Kaduna, Nigeria in August 2014. The intended Nigerian audience is approximately 50 operational-level Nigerian Army detention facility commanders and staff personnel.

Nigerian interest in FMS purchases through the Excess Defense Articles (EDA) program. (FOUO) The Nigerian Navy has had great success in purchasing needed vessels through the EDA program, most notably USCG Cutters *Chase* (now NNS *Thunder*) and *Gallatin* (now NNS *OKPABANA*, transferred to the Nigerian Navy on May 7, 2014, in Charleston, SC). Most recently, the Nigerian Army expressed interest in purchasing several EDA equipment items, including 5x rotary-wing assets (2x gunship, 2x transport, 1x MEDEVAC); up to 50x HMMWVs; and up to 60x Mine-Resistant Ambush-Protected (MRAP) vehicles.

C–IED Training: USAFRICOM has received $3.5M in TSCTP funding, to be executed through Naval Forces Africa (NAVAF), to support the training of Nigerian Army Explosive Ordnance Disposal (EOD) instructors at the Nigerian Army Engineer School in Makurdi, Nigeria. The Navy International Programs Office (NIPO) is coordinating the transfer of equipment to enable NAVAF to execute the program effectively.

Civil-Military Operations: USAFRICOM, through the Special Operations Command Africa (SOCAFRICA) Civil-Military Support Element (CMSE) in Abuja, has been working with the Nigerian Army (NA) Department of Civil Military Affairs (DCMA), which serves as a coordinating and advising body for the Chief of Army Staff (CoAS) on civil-military relations. These efforts include CMSE support to Nigerian Army development of Civil Affairs doctrine as well as planned training for Nigerian Army Civil-Military planners and advisors deployed to each of the seven NA divisions.

USAFRICOM has received $1M for Nigeria Civil-Military Operations (CMO) development through the State Department's Trans-Sahara Counter Terrorism Partnership (TSCTP). The engagement plan includes two primary streams of training:

1. Training in CMO for the currently untrained CMO planners at the divisions is planned to begin in late June 2014 and continue through the end of 2015.

2. Training in CMO for a pool of existing instructors at several Army training institutions, based on CMO doctrine and curriculum. This would begin in late 2014 and continue through the end of 2015.

NASOC: USAFRICOM, through SOCAFRICA, has been providing an advisory element to the proposed commander of the Nigerian Army Special Operations Command (NASOC). The new Chief of Army Staff has placed NASOC development efforts on indefinite hold, citing several factors including ongoing offensives against Boko Haram; however, engagement efforts with the vetted units are continuing in earnest awaiting resolution of where they will now fall in the Nigerian Army structure.

GSCF: DOD and DOS have collaborated to develop a $40M Global Security Contingency Fund (GSCF) assistance program to train border security forces in Chad, Cameroon, Niger, and Nigeria, to disrupt Boko Haram's largely unfettered movement back and forth across regional borders. The Multi-National Joint Task Force (MNJTF) Lake Chad is the most viable organization with which to engage and is the focus of U.S. efforts. DOD anticipates the proposal being notified to relevant congressional committees soon, and we look forward to collaborating closely for approval of this important initiative.

Summit Outcomes: Discussions at the May 17 summit were in keeping with the themes of a regional approach utilizing the MNJTF Lake Chad.

—Participants agreed that over the medium term a coordinated program for economic development in the region is required. The Lake Chad Basin Commission (LCBC) might play a role in these efforts.

—The Multinational Joint Task Force, a part of the LCBC, was also suggested as a vehicle for enhanced regional security cooperation and assistance. This will be pursued; however, Cameroon is not currently a member of the MNJTF.

Question. U.S. Cooperation with Foreign Governments.—The continuing challenge for the United States is that our efforts will have to be creative and coordinated, not only with a partner in Nigeria who is reluctant to do so, but with regional neighbors who have much to lose if this violent militancy spreads, as reports indicate it can.

♦ What is the state of U.S. cooperation with neighbors in Niger, Chad and Cameroon and set it against the domestic capacity of these three countries to address the border security threat as well as the respective governments efforts to address internal tensions that may mirror Nigeria's current situation?

♦ How have we utilized the Trans-Sahara Counter-Terrorism Partnership and other Countering Violent Extremism and other CT programs in the region to address the growing Boko Haram threat and how are they to be augmented if at all? What office or vehicle for coordination exists to harmonize such regionally significant programs as CT–CVE?

Answer. The United States has experienced good counterterrorism (CT) cooperation with Chad and Niger, although their focus has been on CT threats elsewhere in their countries where the AQIM threat has been, until recently, more visible and more direct. In both cases, Boko Haram has been viewed as "Nigeria's problem," presenting only a limited and localized threat to their own security. With the group's expansion this perception has changed and, along with it, we are seeing a willingness to reallocate security resources away from other missions and toward Boko Haram's operating areas along their respective common borders with Nigeria. In short, both countries are capable, and their will to counter the Boko Haram threat is growing, but both also lack adequate resources. With respect to Cameroon, DOD's cooperation with Cameroon is also robust, but regional collaboration is hampered by strained relations with Nigeria. Like Chad and Niger, Cameroon was slow to acknowledge the threat of Boko Haram, but fully recognizes it now and is dedicating national resources to control its border with Nigeria more effectively and to conduct operations against the group. Also, like Chad and Niger, Cameroon has capable security forces that are nevertheless resource-constrained and overextended. To capitalize on this increasing awareness of Boko Haram as a regional threat, the United States has developed a $40M proposal under the Global Security Contingency Fund authority designed to build all four countries' respective border security capacity. Along with our interagency partners, DOD will continue to seek opportunities to promote and materially support regional collaboration, cooperation, and deconfliction of efforts against Boko Haram. The Trans-Sahara Counterterrorism Partnership (TSCTP) is a State Department-led mechanism by which the USG coordinates support to regional efforts to contain, degrade, and ultimately defeat AQAA, including Boko Haram, in the region. Although Nigeria only recently became a TSCTP partner, DOD has received $1M in TSCTP funding to help establish a civil-military operations (CMO) capacity within the Nigerian military, including establishing organic Nigerian capability to train and sustain CMO skills into the future.

––––––––

RESPONSE OF ALICE FRIEND TO QUESTION SUBMITTED BY SENATOR JEFF FLAKE

Question. U.S. Cooperation with Foreign Governments.—I asked a question regarding the ability of the United States to cooperate with the Nigerian Government in the security sector and though a response was given that there are restrictions on U.S. assistance in law, including the Leahy amendment restrictions on the provision of assistance, training, and equipment, you did not discuss the exceptions and waivers associated with these restrictions.

♦ Please describe the legal restrictions, as well as any waivers or exceptions allowed by the so-called "Leahy amendment." Have any waivers or restrictions been utilized under these provisions in Nigeria?

Answer. The DOD Leahy law provides that DOD appropriated funds may not be used for training, equipment, or other assistance for the members of a foreign security force if there is credible information on a gross violation of human rights. The Leahy law also includes two exceptions and a waiver provision to the general prohibition. The exceptions apply if the Secretary of Defense, after consultation with the Secretary of State, determines that the government of the proposed recipient country has taken all necessary corrective steps; or if the equipment or other assistance is necessary to assist in disaster relief operations or other humanitarian or national security emergencies. DOD does not believe that the Nigerian Government, to date, has met the requirements to apply the first exception in that it has not taken meaningful corrective steps to address the problem of gross human rights violations or to identify and discipline those responsible. The waiver applies if the Secretary of Defense, after consultation with the Secretary of State, determines that such waiver is required by extraordinary circumstances. Although the current circumstances in Nigeria are certainly extraordinary, we do not believe they are of such a nature as to warrant use of an exception to, or waiver of, U.S. human rights requirements. Further, even if Leahy restrictions were waived or excepted from, DOD believes that other factors, including corruption and a pervasive lack of political will, would still inhibit building the capacities that Nigeria requires.

DOD has not, to date, relied on an exception or the waiver provision to the general prohibition. To pursue such an exception or waiver, a Combatant Command or Office of the Secretary of Defense (Policy) office would prepare and coordinate a proposal for Secretary of Defense consideration and decision.